DESAVYOK ELFHAME TAROT
Special Edition Guidebook

DESAVYOK ELFHAME TAROT
Special Edition Guidebook

By
Robin Artisson

Illustrated by
Larry Phillips

Layout by
Aidan Grey

© 2017 Robin Artisson. All Rights Reserved. This book or parts thereof may not be reproduced in any form, stored in any retrieval system, or transmitted in any form by any means- electronic, mechanical, photocopy, recording, or otherwise- without prior written permission of the publisher, except as provided by United States of America copyright law.

ISBN-13:
978-1548077945

ISBN-10:
1548077941

BLACK MALKIN PRESS
Concord, NH

www.robinartisson.com

This book is dedicated to Larry Phillips,
Or as I know him, Tharn- my artist and my ally
And his life-friend Morpheus.

CONTAINED HEREIN

Introduction (i)

I: The Narrative of the Mysteries
As Revealed in the Major Arcana
Sequence (1)

II: The Suggested Card Meanings
For Readings (109)

III: The Counsel of the Cards (155)

IV: Methodology: The Oracle
And Vision of Cartomancy (167)

Introduction:

The 22 Panels of the Sacred Tapestry of Fate

The traditional Tarot depictions of the Greater Mysteries (the 22 images of the Major Arcana) present a complete cosmology for human experience. To say that they are cosmological images is another way of saying that they are depictions of discrete aspects of Fate. Fate is a name given to the indestructible and fundamental forces and relationships that make our world what it is and our persons what they are, in a timeless and lasting sense.

If we wish to depict the cosmos or the fateful world as a tapestry, these 22 images of the Major Arcana might be considered the dominant panels of the tapestry, arranged so that their many overlaps and connections are visible. They relate to one another in many surprising non-linear ways, but they also tell a story that can be told in a more-or-less linear fashion, too, following the numbered sequence of the cards.

The value in reading this linear narrative created by the Major Arcana cards is immense, and we shall commit ourselves to that task (among other tasks) in this present work. The only thing we must bear in mind as we explore the Greater Mysteries is that they can never be reduced to just one method of understanding or to one method of analysis. They forever act as what they really are: representations of fateful families of timeless power, and all of them relate to all the others in a webwork that transcends easy understanding. We must never allow ourselves to imagine that we have exhausted their mystery or their power merely because we gained one kind of insight or another from them, using one method or another.

The most obvious cosmological structure presented by the Major Arcana is this: The World card, which is card XXI, contains all of the cards numbered I through XX: The World contains those forces, and is comprised of them. She, The World, is "All That Is" because those twenty families of fateful forces together represent the many forces that shape us and the world and the many things we might encounter in this world. She is an image of completeness or totality.

The Fool Card, which has no number, represents the "person principle" or the being-principle that moves like a wanderer through the world. The Fool has other shades of meaning, of course, and some light is shed on those meanings in the chapters to come. But for a basic overview, it is valuable to consider Card Zero (The Fool) as the moving principle of an experiencing being as it moves through The World (card XXI). Between The Fool and The World are found the twenty "center" mysteries numbered I through XX: They make up the many landscapes and encounters the Fool will experience in the world.

Within the twenty "center" mysteries numbered I-XX, there are two "halves" or sides. The first half is comprised of mysteries I-X, and these I call the exoteric mysteries. They represent the more ordinary, outwardly-expressed forces that everyone regularly encounters in the course of an ordinary life. The second half is comprised of mysteries XI-XX, and are the "esoteric mysteries", representing forces and experiences that influence every life from the deep and hidden interior of the ordinary world.

In one sense, mysteries I-X are the obvious powers of the world that is Seen, the world that is apprehended with the ordinary eyes and rationalized by the ordinary mind, while mysteries XI-XX are the stranger forces of the world that is Unseen, the world apprehended in extraordinary states of mind or trance, or in visions, or in the experiences tied to powerful events like death or initiation.

Each card on the exoteric side pairs with a card on the esoteric side, making a meaningful dyad or pairing of mysteries. I pairs with XI, II pairs with XII, III pairs with XIII, and so forth. More shall be said and demonstrated of this later. This is the very basic and foundational schema of the Major Arcana as we will be studying it with this book, and with the cards that accompany this book. You can apply this schema to any collection of Major Arcana cards from any deck so long as the imagery is sufficiently within the traditional aesthetics of Tarot to match the cards you have obtained here.

These 22 images descend from a very long and noble artistic heritage, a very esoteric and potent image tradition, that began in and around Europe as early as the 15th century, and in some cases, certain influences on the Major Arcana as they came to be depicted are ages older than that. Those interested in an academic appraisal of the true origins of the Major Arcana images can do no better than to obtain Paul Huson's seminal work Mystical Origins of the Tarot and Ronald Decker's incredible work The Esoteric Tarot. Both books do a remarkable job of revealing the historical and mystical cultural realities that coalesced to create the form and shape of the Major Arcana during the Renaissance and leading up to the forms we meet them in now.

The Major Arcana cards can be used as a potent spiritual tool for many tasks. They can be used as objects of contemplation, to help a person apprehend and comprehend the mysteries they represent in a deep, other-than-rational manner. Engaging in this kind of contemplation changes the soul of the person in many subtle ways, bestowing wisdom and insight. They can also be used as a powerful tool of divination. Both of these uses will be examined in this work and detailed notes will be given towards utilizing them as contemplative devices, but our main focus will be on divination with the Major Arcana.

Divination is an important and ancient art, perhaps one of the oldest spiritual and practical extraordinary pursuits of mankind. The Major Arcana cards can be used to perform many sorts of cartomantic divination, but this work will focus on one and three-card readings, as well as readings of counsel. With such potent depths of symbolism in the cards, even readings apparently as small as these can reveal much, as you shall see. The other kinds of readings you may perform of your own design are limitless in their scope or shape.

This work will also give suggested and traditional general meanings for each card and give meanings expressed for certain types of questions, too, such as questions regarding employment or relationships. A chapter entitled "The Counsel of the Cards" is also given for those who need to seek very direct advice about how to proceed in a dense or difficult situation.

All of these meanings and counsels are meant to be subordinated (in line with a person's level of wisdom or insight) with the intuition of the reader or the person receiving information from the divinatory process. Gaining messages from extraordinary entities or from the deep reaches of oneself can never be a very neat or linear process. It must include an element that flows from depth of feeling, too.

When you hold the Major Arcana cards, you are holding the 22 pieces of a roadmap revealing the cosmological outlay of powers and forces that structure everything, within and without. They are not merely dead, mechanical forces; they are living powers, meaning-filled and meaning-generating powers that together can co-create more living power and more living meaning. They glow with an intelligence that illuminates all of the things we call "mind" and "matter" from within. In our tireless cultural quests for the sacred, with all we've gained and forgotten, these mysteries remain evergreen like forgotten Gods or spirits.

And like actual Gods and spirits, they come to our aid at times and remain seemingly aloof at others. They can be comforting to us, or they can be grim harbingers of difficulties. Part of the necessary discipline that persons who seek to unlock these mysteries will need is the patience and dignity to allow these greater powers to be what they are and to approach them with a genuine degree of awe and reverence. Potent messages and insights can be won from the deep places of the self or the world by a person who internalizes the perspectives we are about to examine and applies them-selves with quiet devotion to the ancient art of cartomantic divination.

The first chapter in this work you are holding will give a very detailed narrative description of the story told by the Major Arcana cards in sequence. Within that narrative, the story of each human life is told from the perspective of the universal experiences and shaping powers that bring each life into being, condition it to be what it is, and what it will become.

But other stories are being told, too: stories about how civilization works and why it seems to suffer so greatly beneath its own weight; stories of how culture and society fundamentally influence people and how spirits in the unseen world react to those influences. The cards tell stories about the love that pulls so many things together and the forces of division that destroy things that have combined. They tell stories about the debts that form between the visible and the invisible. The cards also tell stories about how extraordinary help comes to us from the world beyond our rational experience.

An ultimate point of realization, or a completion for all of these experiences – better expressed as a mysterious but fundamental insight that all of the forces of the world existing together make possible – is suggested in the way these Major Arcana cards complete their story.

It is beyond any doubt that an ancient wisdom tradition is recorded in these cards and is still living among us today. It is only reaching us through these 22 special images and their layers of symbolism, but this is no mean estate for an old mystery tradition to find itself occupying. If it must lack men and women to teach others about it, or if it must lack places of initiation to induct people into its insights, it still possesses enormous transformative potency of expression just through these images that have survived these many centuries.

With the Major Arcana cards as our allies, we are each of us very close to some of the most sublime wisdom of our common past. The images allow each man or woman to come to terms with the mysteries on their own time, through their own efforts. Along the way, they allow men and women to gain crucial guidance for navigating life's many challenges.

Once you have read the narrative of the cards, the sublime Mystery Narrative that reveals so much about the sacred story of life in the world that is Seen and the world that is Unseen, there will be chapters giving comprehensive divinatory meanings and counsel for the cards. The final chapter will be a chapter on methodology, giving detailed instructions on how to contemplate with the cards and divine with them.

It will come as no surprise to most that I decided to utilize the traditional numbering of the Major Arcana sequence as found in the Marseilles tradition. A.E. Waite's ill-advised attempt to force the Major Arcana sequence (as it was known and depicted for centuries) to conform to a more modern astrological schema led him to put the Strength card eighth and the Justice card eleventh in the sequence. This was, to my mind, a great tragedy and it has been replicated by quite a few Tarot makers since his time. There are many reasons of interior Tarot logic, symbolism, and structure for the original sequence to be preferred, and it is the one that you will find here.

It is also worth noting that our Special Edition deck is intended to focus on the Major Arcana cards and their use for divination. In the pursuit of giving readings more scope and depth, reversed meanings have been given for all the cards in this edition along with instructions for reading them with reversals. In more traditional cartomancy (and when dealing with "full" Tarot decks of 78 cards) reversed meanings are not nearly as prominent or necessary. Anyone utilizing our divination guidelines here is free to simply refuse to use reversed cards and focus only on upright meanings, if it is their desire.

The study of Tarot has been a lifelong pursuit for me, and the creation of these cards with my artist and spiritual ally Larry Phillips has been the culmination of many wonders and hopes. He helped me to deepen my own understanding, just as he tells me that our co-creation of the card images helped him, too. From drawing and painting these cards down to every detail, he came to embody their mysteries in ways that I still hold in awe.

Tarot is like a "lingua franca" for the modern occult world. In creating the DeSavyok Elfhame Tarot special edition, this Major Arcana-only version of our coming full Tarot deck, I was given an opportunity to communicate the most precious things that I have come to know in my entire study and practice of "the life esoteric." I have been given the opportunity to communicate through images what can only be expressed by images, and I have been given a platform to write what must be written down. It is my hope that this deck and this book will be the beginning of an important conversation about the very fundamental meanings of things in our human experience and in our other-than-human experience.

> Robin Artisson
> The Fortnight of St. John's Eve
> 2017

I:

The Narrative of the Mysteries as Revealed in the Major Arcana Sequence

0: THE FOOL

0: The Fool

When discussing the narrative story of life, death, and initiation that is told by the Major Arcana, we begin with one of the cards that technically stands outside of the narrative – The Fool. As was mentioned before, The Fool and The World are the two mysteries that stand apart from the other twenty, and yet, in much the same way The World holds all of the other mysteries within Herself, The Fool travels through all of the mysteries and interacts with them. In The Fool, we see the image of the human being who is taking his journey through all that exists. His card image seems to show the beginning of a journey, but it could also represent many points during the journey.

The Fool straddles the ground between being foolish and being wise. If a person disregards things for reasons of foolishness, that is folly. If they disregard things because wisdom reveals that those things should be disregarded, that is quite justified. But which Fool are we gazing upon, when we see him in the traditional image? In the image, he seems as though he is about to walk right off a cliff; he isn't looking where he is going, preferring instead to look at a colorful bird that has landed on his hand. This lack of mindfulness seems to put him moments from disaster.

When we don't live in our senses, when we don't really perceive what is around us, we set ourselves up for disaster. When we allow flighty minds to fall into distraction, we may still have senses, but we are no longer really using them in any significant manner.

This is foolish; the senses are sacred and powerful gifts from the Unseen world, our origin, to us and to all beings who enjoy senses. The proper use of the senses can deliver us to the deepest of truths about ourselves and everything else. This is one of the oldest occult truths of mankind, now lost below the pernicious idealism that infects our modern culture, and which rejects the senses (and the world itself) as limited, flawed, and tells us to look beyond the senses and the world for the "truth."

If the Fool in the image is doing this, he is foolish indeed. He would be the image of the thoughtless, careless, and blind. He's reckless and out of touch, potentially capable of any manner of disaster in his folly. Mistakes will be made. He represents all of us, when we begin the journey through life and the journey into the mysteries that initiation might reveal. We start out in full possession of our senses, but they rapidly become dulled by a world that rejects itself, surrounded as we are by thoughtless, careless people who are dismissive of the most obvious, simple, and tangible things. We learn that carelessness, that neglect.

A dog pounces at the legs of The Fool, trying to warn him of the coming danger of the cliff, but he ignores it. The dog represents our animal instincts, our deeper instincts and intuitions that warn us of so many things and guide us from below the level of intellect and consciousness in many ways. It also represents the *Follower*, the spiritual companion that follows us through our lives, manifesting as it does (at times) in the form of a beast. It is another aspect of our reality that we all learn to ignore very thoroughly. By preferring to enjoy gazing upon the bird as opposed to listening to the urges of the deeper powers, The Fool prefers flighty, non-grounded distractions to what might save him.

On the other hand, how could this image reflect a wise fool? If he is wise, then he is using his senses; he is seeing what is there. He knows about the coming fall. He chooses to look upon the bird because it is wise to do so; the bird in this case is not a distraction but a vital message for him. He isn't ignoring the dog; he knows full well what it warns him of. If he chooses to walk off the cliff, you can be sure the situation isn't what it appears to be, and that his fall will not be fatal – or perhaps it will be, and in this case, *that* was the wisest and best course of action and he chose it knowingly.

The dual forces of Folly and Wisdom are met in The Fool, who can be either. They are symbolized by the two-pronged staff he uses in his journey. The eagle above the Fool in the image is the sign of far-seeing and the ability to rise higher and see any situation in larger, wider terms – one of wisdom's chief attributes.

The infinity sign on The Fool's tunic reveals an underlying truth about every being that moves through the world: ultimately, the journey of life is timeless, lacking a discernible beginning or end when seen in the broader view. Only the narrow view creates the optical spiritual illusion of suddenly existing because of birth, and then being blotted out utterly one day in death. The two prongs of The Fool's staff might also represent the painful paradox that arises between our perception of the limited and the reality of the limitless.

The image shows spring flowers and a butterfly, and The Fool's staff is greening with buds of new life – folly, right alongside wisdom, can bloom freshly at any time. Like the lighthearted spring, folly and wisdom can both be lighthearted, and life in its naturally free condition is lighthearted and wander-prone.

I: THE SORCERER

I: The Sorcerer

The "self principle" represented by The Fool begins the journey of experience through the sensual, tangible world here, fittingly at the first mystery: the mystery of The Sorcerer. The first four Arcana, beginning with The Sorcerer, have to be understood as especially meaningful together. They represent the four capacities or aspects of self that The Fool will embrace and express so that his experience might be complete. The first aspect of self, represented by The Sorcerer, is the vitalizing breath of life, the breath-soul which every organic living being requires to live.

The breath soul, the enlivening and animating air which we receive with our first breath, creates in us the vitality of life. By breathing throughout our lives, we maintain our living beings. It also creates the intellect, which is to say the conscious mind and its power to measure the many parts of the world and analyze them. But that breathy mind, created by that breathy soul, is restless like the wind it was taken from at birth. It wanders much, and has an element of mischief to it. It can express its intellect very powerfully, manipulating things in very deep and complex ways. It can tear the world to pieces with its perceptions and tell countless stories about the parts. The very capacity of speech is a power of the breath soul; speech is the "wind of the body" made into sound, guided by the learned capacities of the intelligence.

Magic words, as used by sorcerers and magicians, are expressions of the breath soul. All words are, but some words are special. In the same way magical words can manipulate the subtle world of spirits and hidden forces, ordinary words can manipulate other human minds.

The parts of the world, categorized and measured by the breath-souled intellect, are juggled about, sometimes wildly, sometimes elegantly, and very often deceitfully. There's darkness here; the stories we intellectualize and tell ourselves (and others) about the world can also deceive us just as much as others. We can forget that the world is a thing vastly older and always beyond any brilliant stories we invent about it.

The Sorcerer – like the mind and intellect themselves – has great potential for performing acts of great good and acts of great evil. The Sorcerer is ambiguous, just as the intellect and mind are ambiguous. All are restless, all are unpredictable as the wind is unpredictable. The surface-level personality and memories that are created and rationalized by the intellect/breath soul are likewise ambiguous and largely unpredictable. The hint of mischief and madness in the intellect and breath-souled mind can and will cross boundaries that should not be crossed, more often than is probably good.

The Sorcerer has used his magic to achieve great power, just as the human intellect has given humans a feeling of great power over so many aspects of the natural world and over one another. In the image, The Sorcerer raises a wand with his right hand, a sign of his will, and he has transferred one of his eyes to the palm of his left hand, representing his discovery of how to see into the Unseen world. He has discovered tricks and tactics to access real power. Horns sprout from his head showing that he has accessed the other-than-human aspects of himself; he can cross that boundary, too, and shift his shape with great skill.

The book before him represents the power not just of language, but of written language, which allows for the creation of new kinds of perception, even new kinds of civilizations. It captures knowledge and hordes it. The triangle before him represents his power to summon things into being with his words. His green tunic, skull, and toad-familiar all reveal that the true origin of his power is in the world of the dead, or the world of spirits.

The serpent below him and the ravens flying above him symbolize the presence of the powerful other-than-human person that made all this possible: The Master Spirit of this world, called by Christian civilization "The Devil", but who is actually the Ancient and Immortal Person who indwells the wind and air of our world, and from whom all breath-souls come.

It was He, supreme in the magical arts Himself, who was the origin of the primal words of magical power, and the first teacher of witches and sorcerers. It was He who breathed the potentials of all human intellect into the first humans, making Him the common culture-teacher and tutelary spirit of mankind. The ravens are his chief emissaries in the world of birds because they are the sorcerers of the winged beings, the most cunning, intelligent, and crafty of birds.

Through their eyes, The Sorcerer who has allied with them can expand his senses to see all things; The Master Spirit sees All through them, and He sees through the other beings who breathe as well. By virtue of having breath inside us that has its origin in the greater wind of the world, something of the Master lives in us, too, and in all who breathe.

The serpent is his primordial form because he isn't just a windy character, but a chthonic one, too, found ruling over the powers of the interior world, or the Underworld. He, like The Sorcerer, can move back and forth between these realms of being seen and unseen.

II: THE SORCERESS

II: The Sorceress

The breath-soul, represented by the previous mystery of the Sorcerer, is the first of the four mysteries by which the Person's self is known and expressed. The second, quite in contrast to the airy breath, is a watery thing: a water-soul, which we will call the free soul (though it is also might be called the wandering soul or the dream soul.) Its origin is not the wild and restless winds of the air above the earth, but the deep, timeless waters below the earth, in the abyss of the Underworld.

The breath soul is mortal; at death, it is exhaled and lost. It depersonalizes after a brief time, returning to the wind that was its origin. But the free soul is of a different nature. The free soul is immortal, having existed before the breathing life and existing after it. During life, the breath binds the free soul to the body; after breath has departed, the free soul wanders away from the finished life and back into the depths of the world, back to the Underworld and onward to whatever further destiny awaits it.

If the breath soul is a thing of the day-lit world, of ordinary consciousness below the bright, all-revealing sun, the free soul is a thing of the surreal, moon-lit world of extraordinary awareness. This card, often called "the popess" or "the high priestess" by other Tarot systems, is associated with the moon for this reason. And in much the same way the breath soul is metaphysically aligned to the masculine, the free soul is thought of in feminine terms. Something of each breathing life comes from "above", from the wind and light of our world, and something of it comes from "below", from the darkness and watery depths below. Each breathing life is a merger of above and below in this way.

The interior world, the Underworld or the world's depths, is inescapably feminine; it is the source of free souls, of the lasting, timeless aspect of all life. It is ruled by great feminine powers, or perhaps it is more fair to say that of all the powers that dwell in that world, traditionally feminine-depicted ones have the most influence. Because each being is, in essence, a free soul that has obtained breath and risen into the daylight of a temporary life under the breath, the free soul represents a connection to the true timeless origin of life. It is the means through which dreams, surreal influences, and the voice of intuition reaches each person during life.

The Sorceress might be any one of the feminine indwelling powers of the Great Below, or she may be a human sorceress who has actualized her awareness of the deep, making the source of intuition and the strange mysteries of the deep world more conscious within herself. She is thus wise in the ways of the deep in a more fundamental way, unlike The Sorcerer who dances back and forth between the ordinary and the strange in pursuit of influencing events through sorcery or magic. The Sorceress depicted in the image is primarily a seeress who has obtained awareness of the deeper truths about many things. Within the human person, it is the free soul that carries the deep truths about the person's very existence.

In the image, The Sorceress is seated before a bog full of strange images (mostly faces) representing the passageway to the "waters below", wherein the primordial life arose. It is the pond or body of water from which free souls are drawn. The toad sits gazing into it; the toad symbolizes those who have obtained the power to dive down below the waters and return at will to the strange source of things, to get "behind the scenes" and to the deepest levels of truth.

The cauldron at The Sorceress's feet represents much the same thing – the vessel of the Underworld that was the source of life, and which regenerates life that returns to it. It is a symbol of those primordial waters, and of the womb of the great female spirit who rules in the Underworld, who is the Great Grandmother of all free souls and traditionally seen as queen over all of the dead who have returned to the Underworld, their natural home.

The cat next to The Sorceress is a traditional familiar of witches, also associated with the moon and the night. It is a creature famous for its solitary and sometimes savage ways. Wisdom can force people to become loners, and wisdom can be savage at times, in what it reveals. The source of real wisdom is the source of everything else. The owl perched above the seat of The Sorceress is the embodiment of wisdom, and the power of night and death, and what comes beyond death.

Unlike the breath soul, which tends to rush back and forth between extremes and is fixated upon alternating light and dark and either/or dualities, the free soul occupies a different place, a different perspective. The Sorceress sits between a black and a white tree, representing polarized forces. Her position between them shows that she is not imprisoned by alternating perceptions but has a place of wholeness or at least strangeness compared to the ordinary behavior of consciousness. She sees differently, and is not bound by the ordinary traps and compulsions that lead people's minds in the ordinary sense.

She is dressed in white, the color of the Otherness or the Unseen World, which is also the color of the corpse. The key around her neck shows her allegiance to the Queen of the Underworld, for whom the key is a primary symbol. The book she holds is marked with an infinity symbol to show that it is the true book of life. Life in the deepest sense is not bound by beginnings and endings but is perpetual and timeless. What is inside her book is the true story of life, a story that can't be guessed out or rationalized by the breath soul and the intellect but which the deeper soul knows within itself.

The Person, represented by The Fool, who is traveling through life, death, and initiation gained his breath soul at the stage of The Sorcerer. Here, he gains his free soul (or better, he discovers that he always had it – the free soul is not gained or lost as other aspects of the person are.) He has two more aspects of self to realize, represented by the two cards to follow this one.

III: THE EMPRESS

III: The Empress

The breath soul (air) and the free soul (water) are two of the essential aspects of self. Now we arrive at the station of the Mystery of The Empress, who represents all of bound-less and beautiful nature in the "green and growing" sense, but also in the sense of stones, hills, plains, mountains, valleys, and the wells and springs that give the waters of the Underworld passage to emerge above the land.

The Empress is the Indweller in the Earth, the Great Queen Below whose body is the earth itself, and whose many children (the free souls of the interior world) emerge into life through her once again. At this station of Mystery, the breath soul and the free soul from before meet the body, the most tangible vehicle of life-expression. The body, the flesh, is a thing of the wood and soil and water, the elements of the earth's flesh formed into another kind of flesh that breathes and knows and interacts.

The breath soul vitalizes the body, keeping it alive through a life-time, and acts as a kind of facilitator for the union of body and free soul. A trinity of powers is formed here which is found in every living, breathing being.

The Empress is the Rose Queen, folklorically called "Dame Venus", because Nature itself is a thing that radiates an overwhelming allure. The strange entities deep below aren't just drawn to express themselves tangibly and inhale breath-souls by the light and power of the wind; the Venusian beauty and sensual intensity of the earth and nature are always and everywhere compelling to them.

The same great Person who indwells Nature is mother to human beings and other beings, and nearly all who come to life through the womb of nature seek union and co-created sexual bliss in some form or fashion. It is deeply embedded in us, this Eros-drive, this Venusian nature. And Nature is poetically the Garden of Venus, the Pleasure-Garden of Earthly Delights, the Green Woman's Garden in which all things blossom and grow and unite and die, to seek the bliss of life again.

All of the biological drives that fill us are products of the elements of this world, of this nature, marks of our heritage in the Mother's body and womb. The giver of our life, this majestic feminine power, is likewise the one to whom free souls return in death, making her the regent of death and the many natural death processes as well. The earth gives in abundance, but it also devours in abundance, taking power back into itself to fertilize itself.

On the Image, the Venusian Queen sits on her rose-throne, a throne of dark stone with a yonic shape suggestive of the passageway into and out of the womb. Hares (representing overflowing fertility) leap in the beautiful meadows behind her. To her left and right are two of the Grey Women, the spirits who are bound to her power, bound to her person, and who serve her unimaginable will and impulses by giving and taking life from individual beings and even affecting the health and thrivingof whole families, communities, and sometimes nations.

The Grey Women, the serving-daimons of the Great Mother, mediate her many gifts of tutelage, as well: they instruct in herbalism and wortcunning, in healing arts, in poisoning, in seership, in sorceries and magics that only the most primal powers possess. They are the "Fayerie godmothers" of individuals and families, the entities who give warnings of disasters facing persons or families they are bound to, who protect members of families, and who deliver the "cord cutting" of death when the Fateful forces demand it. Life and Death are both in the hands of the Mother and these dark feminine forces that are agents of her timeless will. In this sense she is the "Fayerie Queen", the Fateful One, beautiful and terrifying by turns.

The Empress, the family of powers surrounding her, and the entire sensual realm of the earth and nature has been subjected to heartless and unimaginable torture, defilement, and exploitation at the hands of insane human beings. It is gazed upon by most humans this very day with condescending eyes. Nature has been desacralized and its sacred forces ignored, but these powers still rule us from the deep no matter how much our modern world may ignore them or believe that Nature exists only as a collection of inert, senseless resources put here for "our use."

The civilizational assault on the Mother, and Nature, and the unjust treatment of the women of our world (for these three things are linked together at the deepest level) is underpinned by a singular mad impulse to claim, own, and control the true source of beauty, pleasure, life, and power which is the Land itself – the body of the Mother, the source of all life within and without.

IV: THE EMPEROR

The fourth aspect of self-being is met at this station of the Mystery narrative. The breath soul (air), the free soul (water) and the body (earth) have been elucidated. Here, the interaction of the breath soul, free soul, and body (their ceaseless blending and "inter-folding and frictions") create the heat of a fire, the fire that we experience as our will. Will does not belong to "us" alone; it is sometimes driven by the biological urges of the body, sometimes by the intellectual strategies of the breath-souled intellect, or by the stranger, more indescribable urgings of the free soul. Sometimes it is created and driven by a combination of those things, or by the influences of other beings and powers entirely.

This truth about the will, that it is not a singular and hyper-personal matter, but a drive, a motivation created by the interactions of many forces within and without us has long ago been forgotten or rejected by our world. It has been exchanged for a more simplistic, ego-centered model of "free will", an idea that will emerges from each person based on their clear and unadulterated conscious wants or choices. It is not so, but the modern and idealized concept of "self" – and the unsurprising hyper-individual focus that toxically emerges with it – came to be a socially accepted reality for nearly all societies after a point, most especially our own.

Will drives us and motivates us in many directions. When understood as systemic, as co-created by many forces within and without ourselves, things are more nuanced and clear. When understood as belonging to us alone and bestowing upon us a power to act completely free of any outside influences, it becomes very dangerous. The very thing we call the "human individual" is a composite thing that emerges from the combination of the breath soul, the free soul, the body, and the will. Outside of those forces (and whatever condition they might exist in) there is no way to know of a self or a person in the ordinary sense, inside the world of living beings.

The Emperor is the very image of the will, but especially of the will grown toxic and power-hungry. He is a warning about power and authority, a warning that humans have yet to heed in any significant way.

For the will that all humans express did finally (individually and collectively) reach out and attempt to conquer the world and conquer other persons, human and other-than-human. Civilization itself made this dark unleashing of the will possible on the largest scale; the creation of authoritarian governments and states, large enough populations for armies and professional classes of soldiers, and stratification of wealth set the stage thousands of years ago, a stage that is soaked with blood still today.

The will in its ordinary state intends to be the "conqueror" of one's life. It intends, in most people, to control what needs to be controlled, to obtain what needs to be obtained, to distance oneself from what is undesirable and make oneself closer to what is desired. If one allows the activity of the will to egocentrically and pridefully run amok, as though it were a thing separate from all other things, it will do as the armies of Emperors and kings have done for ages upon ages: lay waste to the world and the beings therein. The "world" of your life will be wasted; the people in the world of your life will suffer. You will suffer, too.

The image of The Emperor shows the proud conqueror on his throne. Unlike the organic, curved, oval throne of The Empress, his throne is geometric and angular, connecting it to the cunning strategies of the all-measuring and artificing breath soul. The signs of horned beasts crown the throne and adorn its armrests, the horned beasts being signs of aggressive strength and vital power. The land around the conquering Emperor is blasted and lifeless, the cost of his destructive wars and ruthlessness.

His sword and shield are at his right side, his shield well-marked by the swords of foes that are now conquered. To his left are the piles of weapons once used by his defeated enemies. His authority now reigns supreme, but he rules over a blasted world, for authority and authoritarianism as a whole leaves nothing but waste – spiritually and physically – in its wake.

The unbalanced will of this Emperor, as with nearly all historical rulers of great fame, doesn't come for The Empress (who represents the land and the organic treasures of life) with the respect and reverence that is her due, nor does it come with prudence, moderation, or grace. It comes to force, to control, to take, and to use, without regard for the well-being of the conquered.

V: THE POPE

V: The Pope

The story is known so far: The Fool, representing the person-principle who will journey through the worlds seen and unseen, is an entity from the deep – a free soul – but he emerges through the body of nature as a sensual expression of that entity (expressing a body) which gains breath and a breath soul from the wind and air of the world. Then, his will emerges as those three forces converge, and a life has begun.

Where does this life find itself? Within the human social world. And within that world there are rules, laws, traditions, customs, many things to learn, ways to conform, stories, and the entire massive tapestry of social conditioning. There are authority figures whose task it is to transmit this conditioning, this learning and teaching, to every new member of society and to reinforce these norms in members of all ages and life-stages. These authority figures, these teachers, lore-keepers, and instructors, are symbolized by The Pope.

The Pope, naturally, is the image of the teaching authority of the Catholic Church, the church that was fundamental in the creation of medieval European society. Had our Fool been born tens of thousands of years ago in the pristine wilderness of Siberia, the "teacher authority" figure would have been some tribal shaman or elder who passed on the stories and valuable lore of the tribe to young members. Had our Fool been born in 300 BCE in ancient Britain, the teaching authority might have been a bard or a druid or a wise elder, who communicated the same kinds of stories and cultural lores to other members.

The Pope is the traditional image of teaching authority in Tarot because of Tarot's historical origins in the late middle ages. Pope, bishop, and priest were the face of social norm-creation, social morality instruction, and the enforcement of conformity to the principles of Christian culture. But every culture – ancient or modern – has ways of teaching and shaping its members to conform to the normalcy envisioned as ideal by the culture. Every culture, even secular and modern cultures, rely heavily upon conditioning members to conform to many expectations. To step outside of those expectations is to invite social sanction.

In this stage of the mystery-narrative, the person moving through life's mysteries comes under the power of social life, becomes shaped by the norms and expectations of their culture. They become educated by the parents, teachers, professors, and intelligentsia of their culture. The Pope represents the teachings and systems of conformity that specifically apply only to the exoteric layer of the culture; esoteric mysteries and teachings are hidden, not just freely given to everyone.

And in the human social world, the habit of conformity, the will to conform, comes with countless dangers. While a certain degree of conformity is obviously necessary to stabilize a person among their peers, too much conformity leads to the same kinds of horrors and devastation that we saw the will committing upon the world when it became unbalanced, in the previous card.

While The Emperor conquers with swords, the lords of conformity conquer with words, guilt, shame, and talk of social or civic duty. And while the bodies of The Emperor's victims are pierced by arrows, spears, and swords, the souls of people locked under the rule of the conformity-lords are pierced just as savagely by rules and doctrines.

The medieval Church is the best example of the horrors that dwell in the house of spiritual imperialism and spiritual authoritarianism. In the image of The Pope, the symbolism is plain. The walled city behind the Pope represents the human social world itself and civilization as a whole. The richly dressed Pope gives his sign of benediction to his eager followers and acolytes to his left and right – priests who have received his teachings and adhere to his creed. Through him and his bishops they have gained clerical spiritual and social authority. But they have the heads of sheep – for they are pitiful conformists, simple followers, who only feel safe in the presence of the authoritarian shadow of the shepherd's staff.

At the Pope's feet, the dark truth that underlies organized religion and obsessive social conformity is revealed: a bag of gold spills its treasure, and a bloody knife lies on the ground next to it. Violence and wealth-acquisition for social elites is what lies at the secret heart of both spiritual and social conformity. The common people conform and behave; they believe their leaders and authorities to be holy or benevolent, but behind the scenes, the powerful become wealthier and more powerful and they destroy any who don't conform. Those who challenge their clever, venerable racket seldom last very long.

A deep warning stemming from the entire history of civilization rings out here; the crown and the altar, the Emperor and the Pope or the temporal and spiritual authorities of any society, are in unholy wedlock with one another. The imbalances in one are always found in the other; the crimes of one belong to the other. Just so, our own personal or collective wills are often in unholy wedlock with our unquestioned social conditioning.

VI: THE LOVERS

VI: The Lovers

We have seen in the previous mystery station how social conditioning becomes one of the primary forces acting on any person. But social conditioning comes largely from the complex machinations of human beings, which to be fair also sometimes have their roots in other-than-human forces.

However powerful social conditioning may be, it is met by vastly more powerful conditions and influences from Nature and the biological human organism itself. The powers of lust, attraction, and love, these great forces (ever more ancient than human beings) drive all of the varying parts of the world together into blissful sharing and co-creation, exerting their great influence at all times and in all places.

These familiar-yet-mysterious powers are represented as a singular family of forces by this card, and called for lack of a better term "love" or perhaps "desire." This force is seen as one of the true "prime movers" of the cosmology revealed by the Tarot mystery narrative; the only force quite as strong as this one is found in its "twin mystery" on the other side of the sequence of the Arcana: Mystery XVI, The Ruined Tower. The Tower shows the cosmic power that separates things, which severs and destroys things that have come together.

Love, or this power which brings things together on many different levels (from the lust that drives to conjugal union, to the affection and soul-deep love that binds family and friend and kin) has been the subject of much devotion and veneration within human history. The idealization of this force is probably one of the most unwise distortions of reality that humans have ever embraced. For love comes with a very intense side, a dark and painful side, as you might expect considering its twin The Ruined Tower. When love is summoned – or when love chooses to be present – its darker aspects always accompanies it.

People who insist on seeing Love in its idealized, simplified form have a lot to learn. There's no denying its pleasure or its importance to the cosmological health of all things. It deserves the praises it has won, but it also merits the note of its darker side. None can hate one another so thoroughly as those who once loved each other. And even the parent who loves a child more than life itself comes to realize the dark side of that love: to be in the grip of that love is to know great fear.

In the image, we see a traditional image of man united to woman by the power of the lust and love daimon or spirit above. In ancient Greek polytheism, Eros (the son of Aphrodite/Venus) was the daimon/spirit who shot the arrows of lust and attraction into men and women, driving them into one another's arms. The potentially devastating power of this arrow-shot was not kept a secret in the stories of the ancients. In our depiction, the spirit who represents the Indwelling Person of Love or Attraction points towards the union of this man and woman, placing his otherworldly seal upon it. Though a man and woman are depicted here, they represent any two parts of the living system of life that might come under the power of attraction for one another.

No one chooses to feel this subtle and powerful force. We don't choose who to fall in love with nor what things attract us. In the face of Love, we come closest to understanding what it means to live in the hands of a greater power, in the hands of a Fateful force. It is wisdom to submit to this uncomfortable lesson because it will have its way regardless of nearly any other factor.

The great spirit on the card holds the traditional arrow representing his power to suddenly strike beings with lust or attraction. It is bloody to remind us that love's urges are passionate but can turn dark and violent at a moment's notice. What begins in the "fairy tale" of love can end in a nightmare. The spirit himself is horned, showing that he isn't only human and this power binds more than just human beings. Non-human animals, and even spirits and stranger beings feel this power influencing them at various times.

The Tree of Life, and the great spirit of life (represented by a serpent, his most primordial form) are prominently pictured in the image. The Love/Lust Spirit is, in another way of understanding, Him. Life moves and unites and proliferates in the activity of this great power. Life lusts for life. Life seeks great bonds and intimacies with life.

VII: THE CHARIOT

VII: The Chariot

Now the greater picture is coming clearer. The ten stations of mystery that comprise the phenomenal, ordinary world are beginning to come together. The person-principle now goes with breath soul, free soul, body, and the will they create together, all under the power of social conditioning and under the influence of nature's instincts and conditioning. Now we face another factor in the experience-adventure of life – the stranger and more distant Fateful forces that influence us onto one road or another.

But before we meet those strange and distant ones, we have to comprehend that the "going" of the person-principle is what is summed up at this point in the mystery narrative. It is the reality of going to and fro, of having motion, of moving down one road or another, through one situation or another. We have discussed in detail six distinctive powers or families of power that exert so much influence on how the person encounters the many things they will experience. Now we consider the full package – the previous six powers in combination – as they move down life's Fateful highways and by-ways.

The Chariot, of course, is a vehicle that moves down roads and paths. It is drawn by horses, an important symbol that we will return to shortly. Chariots probably didn't appear much in medieval or renaissance Europe, but the idea of a vehicle drawn or given motion by multiple powers (a driver and other beasts) is important.

The Chariot refers to the person as they move down the pathways of their life-time. The horses that draw The Chariot are the breath soul and the free soul – one's intellect and reason, alongside one's emotions and intuitions. The body of the person is itself The Chariot's frame. And the will is the "driver", but we must again and always remember that this driver-will does not pilot the vehicle from a position of complete disconnection or freedom. How it drives has everything to do with the power of the person to reason, along with what they feel, what they intuit, and even the different ways biology may influence them.

As you might imagine, The Chariot's course is shaped by social conditioning, too; it is also shaped by the mad and wild passions and attractions of love, lust, and desire. And when we arrive at this station of the mystery, we encounter another force that shapes The Chariot's course: the destiny of the stars.

There is an ancient reference to astrology encoded into this card, in traditional terms. Astrologers assert that that formations of the distant heavenly bodies – stars, planets, and other such celestial forces – exert an important influence on the course of every life. In terms of The Chariot mystery, the "stars" are references not just to purely astrological or celestial phenomenon, but to stranger, more distant, more deep powers that surely exist and influence all things.

These are the unknown Gods, the unknown Fates, that swirl through the dark mystery of life, through the seen and unseen. They are properly aesthetically depicted as distant and thus, celestial. They are represented as distant lights still exerting a pull and fascination over us. It is not an accident that the "twin" of this card is XVII: The Star.

All sorts of journeys, progress, movements, and trips might be taken in the forest of life. Few can ever know the full story behind why they end where they end, or begin where they begin, or progress as they progress. The breath soul's ceaseless rationality can only attempt to construct a linear story based off of the most obvious forces that come to bear.

This mystery covers not only exoteric journeys and movements and transitions but esoteric ones, too. In our Tarot image, a witch (someone with the power to consciously detach the free soul from the body and move invisibly into the Unseen world thereby) stands between the two horses of her two souls. They "drive" her in any Fateful direction on the surface of the earth, but above her, she has "fetch flown" – shimmered or projected herself in a free-souled shape, to fly above and below.

The stars above her are shaped into the constellation of Ursa Major, the Great Bear, also called by modern people The Big Dipper. In Northern and Northwestern European star-lore, it was "The Wain", the wagon or chariot of the ancient Gods, most centrally Odin, the wind-indweller and sorcerer God as he was known to the ancient Heathens. It is a sign of celestial motion in perpetuity, always circling and pointing to the Pole Star that represents the centralization of a person-principle, for we always experience ourselves as though we were at the center of all things.

VIII: JUSTICE

VIII: Justice

The esoteric anthropology of the person, including rich descriptions of the many layers of causality and influential forces that shape each person's destiny, have been well described. At this point, we are near the end of the "I-X" sequence of the cards, the first ten stations that describe the structure of the entire world that is seen, the phenomenal world or the world of ordinary experience.

There are only two more factors that must be described, two more families of Fateful power that impact and bind every life in this world. While a human person moves under the influence of social conditioning and natural forces every day of their lives, they are also subject to two other major forces: the force of consequences in line with actions and the force of aging and maturity.

The force of "consequences in line with actions" – which binds all things deeply – is what we must discuss here. This force, or this family of forces, is represented in the mystery sequence by The Justice card.

The idea of Justice has undergone a long history of warping and idealization. The distorted form that we know it in now has only a tenuous connection to its origins. Justice was not originally a concept, but a person. She was the Titaness Themis among the ancient Greeks, an ancient divine being, older than even the Gods of civilization. Though civilization came to credit Themis with being the origin or enforcer of the "proper" way of doing things, of adherence to traditional customs and notions of right procedure, an earlier view of this entity shows her to be the guardian of the primordially-allotted boundaries or primal divisions established by Fate. She was the guardian of the allotments made by Fate to every person, place, power, and entity which gave them their rightful and sacred place within nature.

To violate the Fateful boundaries around things – to cross them when it was spiritually unlawful to do so – was to invoke wrathful entities, vengeful ones whose task it was to harm the boundary-violator, thus paying the debt incurred by the violation and upholding the integrity of the natural system. Those vengeful daimons or beings later become embodied in the Goddess Nemesis, who was also called Adrasteia, "The Inescapable."

Actions have consequences. It seems fairly trite to say it, but it's important. Most people comprehend this simple idea on the surface, but few can take the notion of consequence as far as it might need to be taken in a densely layered, interconnected world.

Primordially speaking, Justice is the idea that there are boundaries rightly laid by nature (which enclose the dignity of persons or natural places) that we shouldn't cross, violate, or exceed, for dreadful consequences await us if we do. Our civilized "laws" might be thought of as complex behavior-boundaries, but they are a poor replacement for the older notion of avoiding over-taking or not trespassing on the boundary between human and other-than-human without respect or wisdom.

A point came when the primordial boundaries were completely violated and overrun by human unwisdom. The dark and vengeful powers invoked by the final degenerate existence of wasteful and sprawling human civilization are now commonplace and everywhere. Our civilization will not survive their spiritual predations for long, even as countless civilizations before us did not. But while we still teeter in our latter days, wondering in our ignorance at why so many things in our world have to be so hostile and hard, our image of Justice herself has become a mockery, a shadow of our imaginations and separate by quite a gulf from the Old Power herself.

This is captured in the image used in our Tarot deck. Justice, who was once depicted as blindfolded (assuring her impartiality) holds scales (to measure truth, rightness, or fairness upon) and a sword to painfully extract from wrong-doers whatever they owe, as revealed by the scales that measure their actions and the moral fabric of their persons.

In the corrupt modern day, wherein Justice is an empty ideal seldom put into action by human social groups, Justice is not fully blindfolded. In the human social world, the idol we create and call "Justice" is not impartial. Behind her in the image, a man mows a huge field of golden grain. Mass agriculture is the prime symbol of human over-taking, the primordial violation whereby humans attempted to domesticate the land and re-shape it for their use, stealing the "gold of the Underworld" in the form of grains. They did this to erect their massive civilizations with all their injustices, wars, and slaveries, and all the over-population that will engender further disasters.

The heavy hand of human law, symbolized by the executed person on the gallows pole in the distance, is also a reminder of what happens when the concept of law and rightness is co-opted by wealth-obsessed, violence-obsessed, and order-obsessed human beings. When humans believe they have the divine right to dispose of the land and all its sacred powers as they see fit, Justice is another power they feel like they can make plunder of till it suits what they wish it to be.

Even as her false image proliferates (some say the actual Goddess herself fled the earth long ago) it seems that deeper powers, dark and potent, still care quite a lot about the stupidities that are done upon the earth and the badly-shed blood and tears between human beings. In the image, even though Justice isn't impartial anymore, her scales are still weighing and her sword is still ready to punish those who violate the primordial principles of natural integrity.

Her scales weigh a human heart against a pile of gold. The heart represents the voice of the intuition or the wisdom-revealing power of the deeper soul, and the gold represents the fruits of a person's life or the forms of their many desires. The scales show which was heavier and therefore more significant (or "weightier") to the person.

Finally, Justice as revealed in this mystery-station communicates to us the fundamental truth of inter-connection. Every action has consequences. Over-taking from the earth means disastrous consequences for all. Insulting another wins you their enmity, which can mean a return of ill favor. Eating poorly means less health and longevity. These things and countless others can seem harsh, but they are easily measurable and understood. They are tied to a deeper chain of connection that we can't easily sense, and they don't always emerge as we'd expect. Some people seem to get away with being nasty to others or living wastefully or wantonly. The mystery of why even those persons must face consequences is found in the surreal twin of Justice, which is XVIII, The Moon, a card of many mysteries that we will get to in good time. In the sense of consequence we are discussing here, Justice is quite impersonal.

IX: THE HERMIT

IX: The Hermit

The final major Fateful collection of forces the person-principle must face as they move through the world is the power of aging and maturity. Moving along through the multi-layered families of forces and persons, being influenced so very deeply, acting and interacting through many turning cycles of the world, the person finally starts to spend the life-power and vitality they gained when the first aspects of the life coalesced and found sensual expression. This waning of vitality, this aging, is another natural and Fateful part of the experience of the ordinary world.

In theory, with the onset of age and maturity and through all the experiences a man or woman may have had, a kind of noble worldly wisdom might be born in them. This isn't always the case, but it's charitable to remain hopeful. The Hermit card presents the reality not just of aging and maturity but of time itself, though not in the same comprehensive sense of "time" as is found in the card to follow, The Wheel of the World. The "time" that The Hermit speaks to is the advancing of the individual life-time, and the inevitable interior confrontation that advancement brings with the essence of one's memories and the meaning of one's existence.

For a point comes when a man or a woman will withdraw, whether it be into themselves, or to some secluded place in isolation from his or her fellow human beings. That withdrawal may be temporary, or for a very long time. A point comes when people feel the need to retreat, to search within, to contemplate, to have a break, or to discover things, even if they don't have a name for what they seek. As significant amounts of life-force get exhausted, the dim-yet-inevitable sounds of the Otherness beyond ordinary life begin to become obvious, even if they only appear as strange, deep feelings or gradual alterations of personality.

Though the passage of time and the growth of maturity is key to understanding this mystery's meaning, it is important to note that the contemplative experiences or the urges to withdraw and find a space of peace and clarity can happen to anyone of any age. Though to be fair, it seems to be more common to people who have made it out of the early stages of youth.

Nine is the number of the horizon or the boundary, and this card – Arcanum IX – depicts an older man (by definition approaching the horizon of life) sitting in dark isolation on a mountain-top, coming face to face with his own being and the world of beings that he is a part of. A single lantern hangs before him – the light of his contemplation. A man-shaped mawkin hangs from the cross-pole holding the lantern, one of his gifts to the lonely spirits of that mountain. The other gift he holds in his hands, an offering bowl that might contain honey or wine, or his own blood. The pole holding the lantern is forked – the forked pole bringing together foolishness and wisdom, as we saw in The Fool card.

Demonic faces hover around the Hermit's head; to be alone is to face what's inside of oneself. The demons are fears, depressions, losses, and regrets that live inside of the Hermit, else they are the spirits of the mountain, testing him by seeing if they can scare him away or make him give up his quest for insight.

Temporary or permanent renunciation of the world, contemplative practices or disciplines, or going off on retreats, spiritual quests, personal isolation all belong to this family of powers. The removal of oneself to wilderness areas or putting oneself in extraordinary situations wherein wisdom or insight might bloom, or really working to get to the bottom of things – all of these concepts likewise flow from this mystery of The Hermit. The birth of the desire for wisdom, or the desire for knowledge of reality at its very depths might be found here. But this mystery always resonates with old(er) age, a sense of waning of outward vitality but a growing of interior life, and a sagely sense of becoming strong at the interior level or becoming insightful.

The Hermit represents the experienced person, who has lost the illusions or glamours of youth, or the person who has seen through the large collective lies and social fictions that bind nearly everyone within his or her society. The Hermit has a personal substance of a deeper, stronger, more stable kind, not the flighty spirit normally associated with the youthful or inexperienced.

X: THE WHEEL OF THE WORLD

X: The Wheel of the World

Now we reach the culmination of the ten families or stations of mysteries which describe the fundamental pylons of the world as it is ordinarily experienced. In the same manner that the final card in the Major Arcana series – The World – holds within itself all of the other cards in any Tarot deck, The Wheel of the World holds within itself all of the cards numbered I-IX: The Wheel of the World is the stage upon which all the ordinary, outward, easily perceivable dramas and actions of life occur. It is the world of births and deaths, of wars and enmities, of families, nations, love affairs, political upheaval, and labors. It is also the world of the circle of the changing seasons, cycles of time and social trends, of mountains, forests, rivers, oceans, and broad sky.

The coming mysteries numbered XI-XX are esoterically embedded within that same outward world of circling time and events; however, they cannot be seen with the ordinary eye in their fullness. They are esoterically "within" or inside of the world that greets the eye, but they are still present, exerting subtle influences from the Unseen. Not all of the people who wander on The Wheel of the World, under the influence of all its obvious powers, will become initiates or people who gain entrance to the extraordinary, hidden side of the world. But some will. And the story of those people – what they will consciously, directly encounter – continues with Mystery Station XI, which we will describe next.

For all the rest of the human persons of the ordinary world, the aging and maturity represented by the previous mystery, The Hermit, leads to their natural and inevitable deaths. Some never make it that far; accidents, violence, or illness end their lives sooner. Either way, the death of the non-initiate still causes the exhalation and loss of the breath soul, the decay of the body, and the departure of the free soul. The free soul of non-initiates will be guided or taken by other deeper forces into the mystery-stations beyond, though their experience of them will be of a different character than the experience of the initiate. Having consciously experienced the post-death mysteries while still alive, the initiate's death-experience is of a different character.

The free souls of those who have not consciously encountered the post-death mysteries will be drawn through them in a largely unconscious, dim, or reactive manner before possibly returning to life through Mystery III, the body of the Empress, to re-obtain breath and a fully conscious will. At that point a new identity coalesces, and all the forces we have described before come to bear on the new life. It then moves around The Wheel of the World anew.

This "reincarnation" belief is common in some parts of the ancient and modern world but not nearly as common in the West. It's certainly not necessary to believe it in quite the linear way I have just laid it out; in the end, rebirth or reincarnation narratives can be interpreted on many levels. Perhaps the simplest way of understanding it is to take it as an affirmation of how connected we all remain to the world, seen and unseen, no matter what condition we occupy.

It is worth pointing out that while some believers in reincarnation believe that the process of being reborn happens fairly rapidly after death and that the totality of human life (and perhaps other life) is a timeless and wearisome sequence of trillions upon trillions of previously-lived lives, the ancients of the West did describe deeper worlds (like the Underworld) and other worlds as potential destinations for free souls after death.

Spending ages upon ages of ordinary time in such places, or spending periods of growth and change that can only be described as "timeless" in those places, is another possibility for what might become of postmortem free souls. "Rebirth" into the ordinary world may not be so commonplace after all. At day's end, these mysteries are subtle and can't be answered with any certainty.

All we must know at this point is that Mystery X, The Wheel of the World, is the representation of time's cyclical-seeming circular passage, the mighty wheel of seasons and natural cycles, which encapsulates and sums up the total powers of the ordinary world of our experience. It is the image of the cosmos. It also reminds us that nothing stays the same and that fortune has a way of increasing and decreasing very rapidly.

On our image of The Wheel of the World, a spinning wheel – one of the implements of the Fateful powers – is marked with the eight signs that represent the solstices, the equinoxes, and the ancient sacred times between them. Night and day divide the card into two, and the wide land, full of hills, trees, and mountains spreads out below. Human villages and farms and castles dot the landscape. On the night-side, a youthful hand turns the wheel from darkness towards light; on the day-side, a skeletal hand turns the wheel from light towards darkness. This is the ebb and the flow of everything we encounter in our lives.

X: STRENGTH

X: Strength

With mystery station XI, we enter the second half, the hidden "other side" of the Major Arcana sequence. XI is the first of the next ten cards, cards XI-XX, which represent the powers of the numinal world, the Fateful powers of the hidden world. These powers are "located" inside or within the phenomenal world and its powers. They operate primarily from within, in our experience – but it is important to note that this isn't an attempt to reduce anything to a personal or psychological state. These numinal forces are just as real as the phenomenal ones and occupy their own world, their own experience-state. They are ancient and objectively-existing powers.

If X (The Wheel of the World) is the number and mystery of the ordinarily observable cosmos, the XI shows that same cosmos (X) but with an extra "I" outside of it. That extra "I" is this mystery, called "Strength" in traditional Tarot terms, along with the Fateful family of powers it encapsulates. They act as a bridge between the phenomenal world and the numinal. No one enters into the conscious experience of the numinal without their guidance, or should I say, no one should attempt this passage without their alliance and guidance. It's naturally possible to obtain other "points of entry" but the dangers would be many without the literal subtle strength and guidance that this card/this mystery speaks of.

Every free soul that gains breath, expresses body and will, and travels through the ordinary world is accompanied by a spiritual power – a spirit-person – from the Unseen. This "Follower" chooses (it is conjectured) to perform this task of following due to having an ancestral connection to the living person, or some other bond of affection or great power. The Follower-spirit is tasked with guiding, protecting, and helping the person as they move through life, though it performs this task from the Unseen, in a subtle fashion. The person doesn't often become conscious of the Follower – or see it directly – until very close to death. After death, the Follower acts as a psychopomp, guiding the free soul onward.

The Follower, also called "The Fetch", appears in two forms: beast (theriomorphic), and human (anthropomorphic). The Strength card is the station of mystery that speaks to the beast-form that the Fetch or Follower might assume, just as a later card (Temperance) speaks to the human form the Follower assumes. In its animal form it mediates strength, protection, and ministers to more practical concerns. A human sorcerer or sorceress becomes capable of sorcery by becoming consciously aware of their Follower long before their time has come to die. By becoming aware of it consciously and beginning a conscious relationship with it, they gain powers from it.

The powers that they gain are subtle things from the Unseen world. This station of mystery speaks to the presence – conscious or unconscious – of the Fetch-Beast, the animal form of the follower, who appears in the annals of folklore as the "familiar spirit" of the witch or sorcerer. The Master Spirit behind sorcery, who is also associated with Lordship or authority over beasts and wild things, gives the candidate mystic/witch/sorcerer the power to become consciously aware of this power and the animal shape it wears, as a special gift. This is a reversal of the usual order of things, for this information and conscious relationship is ordinarily reserved for the dying or the dead.

After this point, this important initiatory awareness-change, the sorcerer or witch is no longer a "two souled" person as most people are, but a "three souled" person – the now consciously-available Fetch (in either of its forms) acts symbolically as a third soul to the empowered person.

When the relationship between the human and this spirit is created, a subtle strength is gained and a subtle ally. The ally was always there, for nearly everyone – only the most wicked humans can lose connection with their Follower – but now the ally is consciously related to and consciously relatable, usually during times of sorcerous works or at times when the spirit asserts itself strongly enough to be comprehended by its human partner, ordinarily to warn the partner of something.

The power to move beyond the ordinary perceptions and dimensions of this world is one of the chief gifts this spirit brings to the relationship it has with the human being. In our card image, a woman is undergoing the experience that will "witch" her, make her a three-souled person: she has shed her blood onto a symbol that represents the doorway between this world and the invisible world, and with the help of the Master himself (standing behind her at a distance) her fetch-beast appears to her. She is a sorceress from that night forward, a witch in the traditional historical meaning of the word – a person who accomplishes preternatural feats with the aid of a familiar spirit.

This mystery station manifests itself in our lives not only when encountering (consciously or unconsciously) our Followers but also other subtle presences or spirits. This kind of contact with something from beyond the ordinary world can take many forms, from actual visions or dreams, to the strong, bone-deep feeling of extra strength, assurance, or confidence a person gets at moments of need or crisis. It is a subtle strength – not a strength of muscle, but a strength of soul – that this card refers to. This card speaks to familiar spirits of all kinds, spiritual allies, strange powers that come from beyond our world and assert themselves in various ways and basic deep connections that can help us to move forward or beyond in extraordinary ways.

XII: THE HANGED MAN

XII: The Hanged Man

The moment a man or woman penetrates the barrier that separates the extraordinary world from the ordinary, when they breach the hedge that separates the Unseen from the Seen with any significant degree of force, hell begins. The breath souled mind and personality, so used to the "normal" world, to the predictability of the life lived thus far, is not ready for the fluidity, the disruption, or the strange new influences that flood through the breach.

No breath soul experiencing the strange powers to such a direct degree for the first time can really prepare for the interior impact it will have on their minds and souls or the external impact it will have on their lives.

This is the first thing that all who move into the Numinal spaces must face: the agony, the fear, and the uncertainty of the true "guardians of the threshold." These guardians resonate with the simple presence of the strange immensities beyond. Most people will turn back and live the rest of their lives in fear or denial of what they encountered. But two kinds of people cannot turn back: those destined to become initiates (including sorcerers or witches who will become proficient in their craft) and the journeying dead of this world.

It may seem ironic, but some of the first "signs or omens of verification" that one has touched the extraordinary world beyond the veil or hedge is the appearance of disruption, misfortune, or trouble in one's everyday life, or within oneself.

When someone faces a real terror, a real hell, they find themselves stuck thoroughly. Like the Hanged Man depicted in the image of this mystery, they can't touch the ground, they can't escape. They are suspended between earth and sky. There's many ways they might go, but they cannot. To go left would mean hell. To go right would mean hell. Forward and backwards are hellish. Above and below are pain and agony.

But like the Hanged Man, who in the image has finally lost his ordinary sight under the influence of his painful and lethal hanging, a special new kind of perception can be born when the ordinary ones fail. On his forehead another eye has opened, representing the extraordinary sight that both the initiate and the dead obtain. A soft light plays around his head; in suffering and death an ecstatic, sacred condition may be born.

Agony, death, passion, and lust all have an overlap. The "angel lust" – the final erection and discharge of semen that occurs in hanged men – was believed to fall to the ground below their site of hanging and cause the Mandrake plant to grow. The Mandrake is one of the chief Venusian herbs, with traditional aphrodisiac uses. Our image portrays them growing below The Hanged Man. Few want to face agony or death, but these things still have a secret fascination for all mortal beings. Some fetishize them or secretly desire them. There is an implication here, also, that new life grows from death.

It is a consequence of the interconnected nature of opposite powers that when one is invoked, the others are never far behind. Just as each birth summons a death, agony can summon insight or passion. We can learn to thrill to pain, to yearn for danger or suffering. When death comes close, lust can bloom right alongside it and often does.

The man in our image was hanged, as many men and women were, at a crossroads, so that his soul might not be able to find its way back to the human community to trouble it. The crossroads represents the place where the spirit world is nearest, so those deceased in that place should be able to make the transition easily or even be drawn into it against their will. There was always a fear in the old world that especially crude, powerful, or evil people could beat the system of death, or that mischievous, law-breaking, anti-social humans would resist "going with the flow" and not move on when they died.

The Hanged Man is the mystery-image of agony, suffering, and helplessness before powerful pains and torments and bad situations. It is the image of facing brutal adjustments or transitions, but some of these transitions are related to the shift between one world and the next, such as trance, soul-flight, or death itself. Some sufferings contain within themselves the seeds of mercies or solutions to suffering, but not all do. You won't know which is which until after the noose is tight, and you find yourself suspended and helpless.

Everything about this mystery station points to the liminal place of being hanged or crucified between painful opposites or stuck in places that there is no escape from. There is little clarity here and much suffering. But as said before, powerful things can be born from it all.

parts, and the free soul wanders away into other ranges of experience in the unseen.

After the death of a person, they cannot be spoken with as you may have spoken with them before; you cannot see them as you may have seen them before. They do not think as they did before (the breath soul is vanished, after all) and they do not exist as they did before as a compounded entity. Death for breathing things is a reversion (from one perspective) to a simpler state, though the world of the free soul – which becomes the new world of the dead – is hardly simple.

Though our culture is terrified over the concept of death, and though mainstream religions essentially play on that fear, offering promises that the personality and "social being" of each person will survive death (in exchange for obedience to dogmas, and the embracing of certain religious social choreographies, naturally) the fear of death is completely misplaced. As we have seen already, the terrors and agonies associated with death occur long before the mystery of Death does. The Hanged Man is, in a sense, what most people think or fear about death – being helpless, suffering, afraid, and all the like. But Death comes after those things. The Hanged Man who hangs long enough will feel his agonies end, and then, Death.

Death, if anything, is a great mercy for those in agony. It is a release from physical pains and troubles and a release from the stresses and fictions believed in by the mortal breath soul. Death cannot anesthetize what pains the free soul may carry, but through it, that same soul is able to move into another condition in a very definitive and irreversible way. This allows us to arrive at what Death truly means for us: it means "Letting Go."

All who die must reach the point when they know and feel, at the soul-deep level, that the time has come to let go. The degree of difficulty they may face in surrendering to it, actually being able to let go of the life that is over, is an important consideration. It would be a hell all by itself to be unwilling or unable to let go when the time comes.

Learning to "let go" long before Death occurs is a very important skill and practice. We have many "practice" deaths before we die, no matter who we are. Situations change, things change, and we look up to discover that a relationship we cherished has died, or a social situation we once enjoyed is gone never to return. We discover that those we've loved have died, or that our ability to live as we lived before is now gone, the situation impossible. We have to let go quite often in life, and our mental and social health depends on our ability to do this, to consent to the omnipresent power of change and the revision of life forces and social forces that it brings.

It's terrifying and hard to let go of things we consider to be fundamental about ourselves or the world, but this challenge never leaves our side throughout our lives. It is as though some secret whisper of Fate is to be found in the fact. It seems as though we are being primed for our own coming deaths, trained for it, or at least given multiple opportunities to perfect the art of letting go. No matter how difficult it can be, it is necessary. The Initiate passing through this phase of the mystery narrative must let go of many things they once thought were real or important before they can proceed on the road of initiation.

Our image of Death is a very traditional image, showing Death as a skeleton, swinging its reaping hook that levels and cuts away all things eventually. The crowns of formerly powerful kings are on the ground, and the limbs of the dead are the limbs of the powerful and weak alike, the ugly and the beautiful, the intelligent and the dull. All must die, and one way or another, all must learn to let go. The complex situation of forces that shape all things simply cannot allow things to hold together "as they were" forever. No mortal resource we command (no matter how impressive the breath-souled appraisal we have of it) can halt this fact of the cosmos.

Death's "twin" mystery in the phenomenal world is Mystery III, The Empress – the womb of nature that gives birth and life. But when that birth and life is invoked, so is XIII, Death, always. III and XIII are the Womb and the Tomb, forever bound together.

XIV: TEMPERANCE

XIV: Temperance

So far on the path of the numinal mysteries, we have met the connecting power that gives the subtle strength to access the Unseen (Strength), we have faced the agonies of the unknown and the strange vastness of the beyond, which renders all helpless (The Hanged Man) and we have been forced to let go of many ideas, beliefs, and cherished delusions (Death.) Now, both the mystic and the wandering dead of this world reach a special place indeed – the place where the Follower-Spirit, who first appeared as a beast in station of Strength, appears as a human man or woman.

This anthropomorphic form of the ancestral Fetch-Follower appears to all who have died or who are seriously approaching authentic initiation. Their help and guidance is needed in both cases. This being has been captured in the annals of folklore in many forms, and even the Christian world has given it legendary standing as the "guardian angel." But this is no theological angel; this power comes from a time before civilization and its religions and from a time before the modern fictions of history.

And at this stage – the station of Temperance – the Follower in its form of human man or woman offers what the person needs most: a donation of power from the Unseen, to strengthen, balance, protect, and bolster the subtle forces acting on and around the person. Whatever real power the traveler has to move, to resist dangers, to find their way at the most crucial times – it comes from this being's good graces and affections. In the Unseen, as in the Seen, we do not get along well or get very far without good support and help from many powers. Invisible hands and intentions bolster us, help us, and preserve us in ways we can't fathom.

The man meeting his Fetch-Bride in our image is naked, representing what he has lost so far in the transformative sequence of the numinal mysteries. His mortal identity has undergone much transformation, and this is represented by the surface level of clothing being removed. Clothing and ornamentation often represent the mortal identity – what we wear on the obvious and outward level.

The cup he holds – representing the vessel of his life and mind, his person-principle – is being filled from the cup of his Fetch-bride, which is a sign of her donation of needed power but also a deeper symbol of a sexual union between them. This is further reinforced by his act of offering her a gift of bread. The bread and wine, the seed and the blood, are symbols of the sexual fluids and the sexual act of union.

The Fetch-Bride, the man's Fayerie-mate, is wearing green, a sign that she belongs to the Fayerie world, the Unseen, the place of the dead. She sits in a leafy bower in a day-lit field, but behind her is a world of starry night. It is a sign that she sits on the boundaries between things and aids in transitions. And what she gives, when she meets her beloved in any kind of exchange or union, is a balancing power that heals or corrects any wounds in the soul, allowing for her beloved to journey onward with the needed strength to face what is to come.

XV: THE DEVIL

XV: The Devil

In much the same manner that the "new" person passed through four elemental stations (Mysteries I-IV) before meeting and being integrated into the ordinary world and the human social world in the station of The Pope, now the person who has passed through the first four numinal mysteries is ready to enter into the extraordinary world and be integrated there. To do so, he must meet the Great Entity who is twin to The Pope, the dark shadow of the human world's teaching authority. This entity is called "The Devil" in the language of Tarot symbolism, and this title was given to him by Christian culture for a very long time before.

The Devil casts a long shadow over Christian culture and became, through convoluted means, a chief figure in Christian myth and in rural folklore. It is important to point out that Christian theology gives us a theological devil who is distinct, in nearly every way, from the folkloric devil, and yet, the two figures are still strangely unified in the minds of men and women living under Christian cultural regimes.

If The Pope represents the cultural authority of the human social world, of civilization, The Devil represents the authority of the world of spirits. The Pope tames people with his teachings and restrictions. The Devil is wild, and he reverts those who pledge themselves to him back to wildness. Despite the names involved, "Pope" and "Devil" are not some ordinary feuding pair of "good and evil." Good and evil have nothing to do with this pairing or what they represent. This is a twinned set of powers that represent civilization and the wild, the tame, and the free, the rational authority of the world that is seen and the trans-rational authority of the world that is unseen.

It is clearly obvious that the Pope and the civilization he teaches, shapes, and represents are both capable of unimaginable destructiveness, slavery, and wickedness. History leaves no doubts. By some reckonings, the wild represented by The Devil is the more attractive option – less damaging to the natural world and free of the restrictions, cultural fascisms, and insanities of the human world.

This station of mystery is where the person-principle meets the Lord of the Night Side of the World. Just as the Lord of the Day-Lit World bound that person with the rules, restrictions, and teachings of the ordinary life, the Night-Side Lord binds the person with a new set of insights and revelations. To go among the spirits means becoming like the spirits. To go into the wild spaces beyond reason and ordinary conception means to become something beyond reason and ordinary conception.

So after receiving the strengthening and guidance of the Follower in Temperance, that Follower guides a person here, to meet the Great Power who has authority in the Unseen, the Lord of the Underworld who is (as discussed before) the Great Person who was the teacher of sorcerous and magical arts to The Sorcerer in the first mystery. Binding to rational restrictions and falsehoods – however useful they may be in a human social world – enslaves us ultimately. But being bound to the strange revelations and patterns of the Unseen world's deeper ecology liberates us.

The man and woman standing before The Devil in our image are witches being initiated according to the pattern given for witch-initiation in folklore. Naked of their surface mortal identities, they pledge all that is in-between their heads and feet to the Great Master of Spirits. This initiates them, makes them reborn to a world of spirits, and begins their transformation into otherworldly beings.

They won't lose their ordinary humanity – not completely, yet – but while they live, they will be hybrid beings, partly of our world and partly of the spirit world. Their ultimate destinies may be shown before them: the two spirits attending the Devil in the ceremony are Hobbs, the wild, part-animal and part-human appearing spirits who are his servants and ministers. They are ministers of the wild and strange who appear to sorcerers and witch-covenants as their tutelary spirits in The Devil's name.

The Serpent that is his primordial form is on the ground between the initiates. The Cavern of the Underworld that they are within is the body of the Earth Mother, the Earth Indweller, the womb of all life where new things are born, and where the dead return to. The Initiates have spiritually died to their lives before, just as the ordinary dead who come here have died in a more ordinary sense.

Civilization has made the ordinary world contrary and opposed to the Unseen world. The binding, revelations, and changes brought by the Devil and his ministers, though they may be powerful and positive in the Unseen, will always be thought scandalous, unstable, and even evil by the ordinary world. It must be thought so; it is beyond the comprehension of the breath-souled bias of the ordinary world. Thus, the binding represented by The Devil in Tarot divinatory terms often includes elements of addiction, being controlled or bound by harmful forces, and even abuse – for the wild is depicted by civilization as brutish and brutal.

The Devil is depicted here in a traditional form: bestial and horned. Civilization condescends to the animal as primitive and unevolved, as the symbol of what it arrogantly believes it has overcome, even though all humans are also animals and all humans live under the influence of animal bodies and instincts. The denial of this fundamental fact of human existence is practically the hallmark of civilization. But the animal, the beast, is the form worn by the primal Gods; they transmit a pre-civilized story of sacredness and power. The Devil's bestial shape means vital power; it means primordial strength and divinity. He is a divine being who was not created by civilized humans or shaped in their image.

There is no progress into the numinal without passing through this dark and transformative stage of the mysteries. Wisdom and insight cannot be made whole without the dark "other side" of understanding, however brutal or strange it may appear to the ordinary mind.

XVI: THE RUINED TOWER

XVI: The Ruined Tower

The traveler through the numinous world has come a long way. Now, moving as they are under the new kinds of awareness, newly bound by perceptions of the ecology of the deeper world (which are Nature's most fundamental laws and realities) they become aware of something dark. They become aware of the deeper debts they owe because of how they lived and interacted with other beings and forces before.

And they begin to become aware of something more disturbing, though every bit a wonder: Love's dark "other side" – the power that fuels separation, hate, and the dissolution of compounded or united things. This dark twin to love, hiding as it was deep within the intense activities of love, is now met face to face. Just as all who are born must die, all things that come under the power of attraction must face and come to terms with the power of separation.

The final and most fundamental illusions about the world and the self are facing extinction at this point. The Devil's tutelage has started a trajectory of growth and re-appraisal of everything, and there's no way that the house the unwise ego built before can survive. Reality is dawning, and it will no longer be a one-sided or self-serving thing.

The Tower represents that high and powerful house that unwisdom built. It was built to keep the ego and all its illusions safe from reality beyond its walls. It was built to maintain a dream-life, which was mistaken for the only real life there was. At this stage in the mystery narrative, that Tower must fall, it must become ruined and destroyed. The initiate or the journeying person has already lost much and undergone many changes; this represents the next major surrender – another potent "letting go" or a second death of types that they must endure.

In the image, The Tower is struck by baleful red lightning shot from the eye of the Master Spirit himself; his gaze will only permit the truth to survive. The fateful forces of destruction and death – the Wild Host – swirl about in the sky above and shriek in lustful satisfaction. The lightning and its destructive fires seem so diabolical and fearsome, but powers that liberate can seem tyrannical from the perspective of those who hold fast to their prisons and identify with those prisons.

From the Tower fall two men. One is a priest, a cleric, representing The Pope and all he stands for: the human social world's religions, conformities, and consensual propagandas. The other man is a king, representing The Emperor, and the governments, laws, armies, violence, and wars that are such a normalized part of the human social world. Beneath both falling men, who have been overthrown by immense forces that are older and more powerful than the civilizations they shaped, stand those to whom they owe repayment for their crimes.

Below the falling priest, a wild beast, a wolf-like monster from the deep forests beyond civilization, waits to devour him. The priest denied the wild, defamed the spirits, labeled them "demons" and destroyed human relationships with them. He must now pay the debt of that. Below the falling king, a rioting group of peasants shout for justice. These are the people the king and his nobles exploited for their labor and on whose backs they lived well, while the poor people lived in hovels. He must now pay the debt of that, of the corrupt and unjust social system that he maintained and enforced. The "ancient regime" – the unholy alliance of throne and altar – is overthrown. The castles they built in denial of what was real, and in denial of basic fairness and decency, are falling to pieces.

The priest and the king represent something in each of us, too. The priest represents our own denial of the spirits and the spirit world, our denied and forgotten duty to the primordial animism or spiritual ecology that still lives at the heart of our beings, just as it lived in our first ancestors long before the curse of civilization. The king represents our own arrogant egos that attempt to over-control everything and make our lives easier no matter the cost to many others, human and otherwise.

The Ruined Tower is the image of the fundamental destructive powers of the Unseen, which break into the Seen World at certain times to extend their holy rage – times when civilizations fall, or when wars lay ruin to the world. It also emerges in individual lives ravaged by hate, violence, or trials of the mind or body that bring things to an end or to separation.

XVII: THE STAR

XVII: The Star

And now, at last, the person-principle traveling through the numinal mysteries arrives at a tranquil and beautiful place, a place that radiates a presence of sublime mystery, ancient age, timelessness, and hope. The traveler has been through many trials to arrive at this point. And here, in the station of the mystery represented by The Star, the traveler awakens to a very special kind of knowledge or awareness that they carried within themselves the entire time.

When we ask the question "upon what does the possibility of hope truly and reliably stand?" we are met with a long sequence of possible answers, all of which fall apart when we recognize that not much is reliable in the ordinary world. Because of the ever-changing flow of forces, the ceaseless coming into being, persisting, and passing away, it's only a matter of time before anything we put our hope in seems likely to disappoint us or dash our hopes.

And yet, we all feel a sense of hope – however vague or fleeting – at many points in our lives. Even in the face of unimaginable adversity or despair, hope finds a way to flicker or even thrive. This points to the operation of a deeper principle or power. Hope – such a precious and sometimes dangerous thing – from the perspective of the mystery narrative can only really stem from one place. And in this card, the initiate has arrived at that place.

The free soul is the timeless principle of life, the aspect of self that pre-exists and post-exists the sensual life we all know now. Its home, as we have learned, is in the deep Underworld, where its substance is one with the substance of the waters below. These waters are symbols of the womb and life-giving power of the Earth Indweller. The Underworld is the free soul's true country, its true origin.

But when the free soul expresses itself in the intersubjective world of breathing beings and moves on the Wheel of the World above, it comes under the power of the breath soul and loses its conscious connection to its surreal and strange home. The rationalizing force of the breath dominates, but the personality that forms under it still feels a deep connection to something mysterious. It feels something it can't name. Memories or impressions of the ultimate home of each being become dormant during a breathing life. They are felt, but not understood or recognized for what they are. Only in dreams or visions can the deeper layers be glimpsed, but not until death (or initiation, or through the mystical ability to visit the Underworld while alive) can they be consciously re-integrated with.

Our hope comes from this single fact. We are beings that belong to a deeper story, to a deeper home, a stranger tale than the one we tell (or get told) about who and what we are here in the world of reason and logic. Some part of us knows of this connection to the deepest places of the world. No matter how bad things get on the surface, something in us knows that this isn't the whole story. The truth is even more intense than we realize; this isn't even the tip of the iceberg of the whole story.

Our deeper connection – even if it is lost to our consciousness and unknown to our conscious personalities – provides a groundwork for an intuition or feeling of hope. In this card, we are treated to a vision of what the traveler sees when he arrives, after his long and hard road, upon the Meadows of Elfhame. These meadows are the strange landscapes of Fayerie-Land or the Underworld. He comes face to face with his true mother, the Great Grandmother of Souls, who is shown in our image manifesting as the Venusian spirit of life and death.

She emerges from the waters that are another form of Her creative power. She points upwards to the brightest body in the early evening sky, which is Venus, identifying herself with that body which is poetically conceived of as a star. Throughout our lives on the surface of the earth, that star has shined down upon us, the source of hope and beauty in the night sky. But this is no ordinary night sky that She gestures to; it is the sky of the Underworld. Yet, that star is still here, because it is Her, and She is here. Esoterically, the pin-points of light in the sky of the Underworld are the "lights of lives" being lived on the surface of the world above, or other powers in the earth or on the earth, shining through and downward where those in the origin-country can see them.

The traveler at this point is exhausted, having lost much through the harrowing encounters with the mysteries represented by The Hanged Man, Death, The Devil, and The Ruined Tower. The path through the numinous thus far has been brutal, terrifying, and deeply transformative. But in much the same way the Fetch-Beast at the stage of Strength helped the initiate to access the numinal, and the Fetch-Mate at the stage of Temperance gave guidance and prepared the initiate with needed subtle power, the Queen of the Underworld here now greets the initiate to offer hope, acceptance, shelter, and to make his awareness more complete. This is a place of respite and regeneration, of having hope re-kindled and strength returning for the final challenges that must be faced.

The Queen reveals the initiate's true identity as a child of Her womb or Her waters, his identity as a member of the Family of the Underworld. Chains of relationship, long lost to the furthest reaches of history and beyond-history are remembered. The larger story becomes more obvious. And the Queen of the Underworld shows him the way to go from this point. Hope is born.

She washes those who come before Her in the waters of memory. It is a purification and an awakening to a deeper and more ancient identity. The Tree of Life grows next to Her pool of souls and eternal nascency. On it perches a bird, representing a free soul that is preparing to fly away, following its own fateful story.

XVIII: THE MOON

A time comes when there's no more hiding, no more ability to put aside that precious little inch you reserve for yourself. A point comes when everything has to be out in the open, out on the table, seen face to face for what it is. For those who have made a habit of obsessively protecting that final tiny inch of themselves, meticulously hiding it from everyone, nothing could be a more terrifying prospect.

It's ordinary to nurture and hide that little portion of oneself. It feels dignified; it feels as though one has a right to something that is "just theirs." But the traveler here in the Realm of the Moon faces a choice now between remaining in the course of the ordinary or gaining something extraordinary. And to gain the extraordinary, ordinary impulses will have to be shed and sacrificed.

The person or entity who has been traveling through the various Mystery-stages of our Tarot narrative has been through many challenges and many transformations. When they came under the initial conditioning of the social group they found themselves in, back in Mystery stage V (The Pope) they had to accept a lot of outside material into themselves, and they had to change to conform to it. But deep down, they protected and reserved their own private sense of self.

Mystery stage VI (The Lovers) delivered them into the hands of a great power that forced them into feelings and situations that they both loved and sometimes hated. But deep down, they preserved their own special core of identity.

Whether they were facing the consequences of living in the breathing world, facing the hard-won insights of eventual maturity, or whether they were suspended painfully between life and death, between pain and pleasure, they protected what they felt was essential about themselves. Death came, and they hung on. The Devil himself might have put his heavy binding upon them, transforming them, but they maintained their most precious kernel of self.

When the great destroyer came in Mystery stage XVI, The Tower (and through what can only be described as a miracle of tenacity) they still held on, albeit tenuously and raggedly, to their most interior storehouse of self-fictions, the joys and the pains and confusions that they identify with so deeply. After The Tower's great lashing and burning, the storehouse might be mostly empty, but a few locked boxes still remain inside.

Now, the Great Venusian One who met the traveler in Mystery stage XVII (The Star) has bathed them in the healing and hopeful waters. Now, the traveler moves on to the place of the final revelation. The last locked boxes will be opened and their contents examined.

The dark, surreal, and frightening country of the Moon stretches out before the traveler. This is the vast and dimly lit kingdom of shadows, the full expanse of the Underworld's mystery. This is the strange country of the free soul, the birth-country of all entities, as it lies behind and beyond the Great Queen's starry bower. Out here, countless living shapes and forms without names move slowly about, slithering or coiling as though entranced in the rapture of dark fantasies. Perhaps they are in timeless contemplations, dreaming of whole other worlds, or just dreaming of things that no language can capture.

The roots of everything occurring "above", in the outward, expressed world, begin right here in this dark ground. And all things, from the echoes of fallen civilizations, to the lost dreams of mortals, to the souls of beings released by death, end up here. And here the circle is made complete. All is to be known, all is to be faced, here in the deep dream of the world.

From the breath soul's perspective, real self awareness or genuine and complete self knowledge is a nightmare. It can't stand to imagine that there were things about the self or the world that it couldn't comprehend or take into account. It can't bear to be thought, in final analysis, a limited thing. The breathy pride hides a breathy fear, and the Underworld becomes presented as a hellish place of tormented forms and dark terrors that must be avoided at all costs.

The Mystery stage of The Moon is a stage of paralyzing fear for just these reasons. The gorgon-like face in the moon shown on the card is a symbol of the terrifying and female-shaped entities that legendarily "petrify" or turn people to stone, a reference to paralyzing and soul-deep fear. But for every secret thing that can't be understood or every weird thing that is terrifying in the dreary landscape deep below, there is a thing that is important to understand and a fear that must be resolved.

For this lunar world, deep below the sunlit world, is not just a place for the dead but the source of life. It's not just a place of fears but a place of joys, too. That we cannot understand this without having our heads dipped in it, and without being forcibly held underwater until the initial panic of drowning passes, is a symptom of our disconnection from our origins and from the world as a whole. The most terrifying experience in the world hides the key to the definitive end of all terrors.

The powers of the World of the Moon aren't ever going to be resolved to us intellectually; they simply can't be. But they can be resolved emotionally to us, and this is the final belonging, the final letting go, the final experience the traveler needs. This it won't happen until the "last inch" the traveler has been preserving and hiding in himself is revealed and known.

In our image, the great and sublime moon-disc glows above, its vaguely menacing and frightening face gazing onto the dark landscape of the Underworld. But it doesn't just gaze downward; it gazes into the souls of all who travel through. A hazy "moon-bow" surrounds her, casting a silvery, ghostly light. This is the face of the Indwelling Queen of Spirits, the feminine tutelary force of witches and sorcerers from time immemorial.

Two wolves bark and howl at the moon, making the sound that has terrified the civilized humans of the breathing world for ages of time – the alluring and disturbing sound of the wild, crying out beyond the borders of civilization's pretensions of safety and order.

The canine entities – whether wolves or dogs – are some of the chief mythical and folkloric attendants of the Underworld powers, particularly the Queen of the Underworld. In one sense, they represent Her personal serving-daimons, the spirits attached to Her retinue. They are the literal "hell hounds" who come from a place of dark truths and consequences, who gnaw at the souls of those who have incurred dark spiritual debts. Their barking being heard is a sign that a person has fallen into the iron grip of these fateful, underlying feminine forces.

In the deep waters of the Underworld, the primordial force of life – symbolized by a great serpent – swims. The snake or serpent, too, has disturbed mammalian mankind for eons, whether it was depicted as powerful and wise or as cunning and evil. Wiser humans have recognized in the serpent's form the primordial form of holiness and life-force as a whole. As civilization's degeneracy proceeded apace, the serpent was left to be nothing but evil.

There the self-replenishing and regenerating power of life sits, ageless, serpentine, and wise. He coils in the waters of life at the heart of all things. There are no more fancy forms to cover the dance of life-force; the serpent is, esoterically considered, the simplest form of life, the primal or basic form of living power that wishes to replicate itself and change its shape in a billion ways. To those who fear the primordial as evil or dangerous, the great serpent is the devil. It is the dragon; it is the leviathan monster of the depths.

To those who have seen below their own fleshy surface at their own serpentine DNA and learned to feel with their own "lizard brains", it is the very ambiguous, indestructible, and all-embracing power of life itself, the Universal Daimon.

Two stone towers stand near the water's edge. One is dark, its door closed; the other is lit from within, its door opened. The closed and dark tower is no longer a concern for the traveler. They have faced what was within, and it no longer stores things that must be dealt with. What remains to be dealt with, what they fear most, is in the other. Their final deceits, their final difficult challenges, the last things they couldn't admit to or face up to, they wait inside. It is a place only they can go.

The last consequences of how they lived above in the breathing world are faced here, for this realm is where the deep consequences of things are resolved and where the real judges of what happens above keep their judgment seats. The (once again) feminine-shaped fateful powers that govern consequences and vengeance and the repayment of debts are met in this landscape, and depending on the state of mind and soul of the one who meets them, they can be very pleasant or very terrifying.

Until the traveler goes to the last door, the journey through the surreal moon-lit landscape will be a phantasmagoria of both resolved and unresolved issues and powers. It will be a place of dream-like visions and delusions, of personal narratives gone wild or turned toxic, of nostalgic joys or regrets still living like traces of ghosts in the soul-memory of the traveler.

These are the terrors and wonders of the soul's night-time, and until the last door is opened, this is how it will remain. When these terrors and wonders sometimes seep upwards into the breathing world, they can invade the minds of breathing people and inflict all manner of inspirations, dreams, terrors, and even madness upon the living.

Travelers through this Underworld region might wander in this strange state for eons of time, for time has no real meaning here. They may never build up the courage to go where they must and thus stay here forever. But some will find that courage, largely because of the donations of power and help received from their many helpers before this point. And then, something very profound awaits them. Until then, no one will see what is real until they lose their fear of what is real.

XIX: THE SUN

XIX: The Sun

Since the dawn of human time, the experience of the bright, warm, life-force pouring Sun has been the fundamental sensual experience that encapsulates the whole of human joy. The veneration of the sun is universal; it is not hard at all to explain why, and the importance of the sun's presence and donation of needful power to the entire cycle of life, is beyond obvious. Even in times when the sun was not worshiped directly as a great divine power, it was still associated with the life-granting and abundance-granting gifts of many divine beings throughout human cultural time.

In the later Christian period the sun was relegated to a mere "created thing" and veneration could only be directed "above" it, to the abstract creator God believed to exist apart from his creation. And yet, the Christian mind still could not separate their supreme being and their supreme sacred value from the aesthetics of light, of day-time, of brightness, and the triumph of light over darkness. The solar aesthetics of idealistic monotheism are everywhere blatant. The Sun has, for ages, been the visible image of God, or of the chief life-giving God or Goddess, depending on the varieties of culture.

The Sun Tarot card is a card that presents a feeling, a lived experience, of great joy. But if we simply said that and stopped there, we would fall very short of the sublime depth and subtlety of this mystery. It does not do to simply associate this mystery-stage with the immense globe of fire that we see and feel in our sky daily or with the historical spiritual-aesthetic associations that have been built around it in the religious journey of mankind.

The Sun follows The Moon in the sequence of the mysteries, and it represents the most profound spiritual joy and liberation that a human being can feel when they have unraveled the "final knot" – the last difficult or terrifying inch they needed to resolve in the deep world of The Moon. In this way, The Sun "rises" to end the difficult night represented by The Moon, but it doesn't rise to drive away tangible darkness with tangible light. The light of The Sun in Tarot is never simply a brightness that disperses darkness; it is an interior light that disperses interior confusion and pain. The special nature of this interior light and what actually brings it about needs to be discussed now.

The fortunate beings who courageously opened the final door in the dark dreamscape of the moon-realm likely had to face all sorts of issues. Whatever was unresolved inside their own minds, they had to face with a kind of honesty and acceptance that is rare these days. But it was all for a reason; the unresolved materials were all standing in the way of a core fundamental awareness that they couldn't have until the obstacles were gone. The nature of this core awareness deals with what it means to exist at all, as an entity who lives, dies, searches, journeys, and has experiences of any sort in the first place.

The secret hiding at the core of all confusions, the unspoken thing that civilization itself cannot bear to admit or even conceive of, and that we who are shaped by civilization can very seldom see or feel, is the secret that might be called "radical relational personhood." Put more directly and artfully, the secret is called "Interbeing."

No matter what our problems were, those things that haunted us or pained us, and no matter what our joys were, those things that pleased us or fulfilled our need to be affirmed as social beings, we still needed our very separate persons to be the royal houses of all those things.

We needed our perception of ourselves as lone, disconnected, and separate persons to be absolute sovereigns of our pains or our pleasures. The idea that our fundamental personhood might be a diffuse thing, a *relational* thing, and not a highly distinctive and separate thing from every other entity out there, was a threat to the great honor of radical individuality.

As painful and isolating as it might be to live under the falsehood that we are all radically separate beings, we come to identify with that pain and isolation and accept it as normal, as part of the baseline of self. When this hurts us or others, as it often does, that strengthens the error. When it satisfies us, when it allows us to lay claim to pride in accomplishments as though only we were responsible for them, that strengthens it too.

But the truth of Interbeing liberates us from the pain of absolute isolative thinking and the concomitant unhealthy ego-construction that follows in its wake. Every self-fiction, before it is examined and faced, is a wall between us and the liberation of Interbeing. It doesn't matter if the fictions are painful or pleasurable or if they are a great ocean of fictions blending both and everything between; they all stand between us and this fundamental truth of our existence.

Interbeing means that your "self" and mine and the selves of every other entity in existence create each other through interaction. This massive system of co-creation doesn't just speak to our nature as entities within this system but to the nature of the system itself.

When everything moves together, communicating, interacting, sharing power, taking power, stealing power, donating power, seeing, being seen, hearing, being heard, feeling, being felt, mingling, co-creating, separating, co-destroying, the world seen and the world unseen are essentially created. Because this system of communication has been going on between powers and persons in a timeless way, the worlds seen and unseen are themselves timeless, without birth or death. Certain aspects of the world we ordinarily see can be destroyed, just as certain aspects of our selves can be destroyed. But the world that we see now, like the selves we experience now, can never be completely destroyed.

And in the operation of this massive system of Interbeing, this ongoing event of great sublime majesty, with all its pains and travails, all its blissful encounters and mysteries, a natural joy emerges. A natural sense that it is right and proper appears, an idea best expressed as "The Fitness of Things."

When the Traveler in the moon-world faced their final self-fictions, their final pains, the forbidden sides of themselves they couldn't face before, they reached the conclusion that these things hindered them from seeing: the conclusion of Interbeing. What they unconsciously feared would mean their own self-extinction didn't actually inflict that upon them; it freed them from the ludicrous notion that they were radically isolated beings, completely responsible themselves for every pain, pleasure, embarrassment, honor or torment they had experienced and internalized before.

They saw how things really worked; they saw the eternal operation of relational existence. They were finally able to be what they really were all along – part of the immense

Interbeing, part of the immense and timeless community of life. Wisdom in them, they realized, came from many other teachers and circumstances beyond their choosing. Unwisdom in them, they realized, came from many other teachers and circumstances beyond their choosing.

Joy in them, they realized, came from many other partners and circumstances beyond their choosing. Pain in them, they realized, came from many other relations and circumstances beyond their choosing. What true share of responsibility they had for various things within a conditioned, relational system, they realized it. What true share of responsibility they didn't have for various things, they also realized.

And they realized kinship – belonging – in a way that is beyond ordinary conception. No longer was their particular form or species the central beacon of importance amid the many forms of life; it was one of many, related to many, dependent on many. No longer was their particular form of mind the deepest or greatest or best; it was one of many, shaped itself by many, dependent on many. The neurosis of isolation is thereby banished forever.

The Sun represents the intensified power of life and mind inside of a realized person, which can finally be what it is, without shame, confusion, self-loathing, doubt, or obscurity. The glowing light of the sun in the sky represents the way the life-force of the liberated person (including their mind, their free soul, their breath soul, and their body) radiates joy at finally being able to be what they are, without confusion, fear, or guilt.

This joy – the joy of consciously knowing ones' eternal belonging to the Fitness of Things – is the secret Sun at Midnight, the light that shines in the darkness. The division between self and world is gone, and yet, the self has not been obliterated. It has become free, wise, canny, and found lasting peace.

In our image, the Master Spirit of this world, the Indweller in our breath and in the vitalizing wind of the world, is depicted as the spirit of the tangible sun in the sky, for he gives vitality and life to all in the same way the sun gives life and warmth to all. Below him, as he gazes down upon the beauty of the world, is a triumphant parade of entities, each of them telling a story of Interbeing.

A young girl rides upon a donkey in the parade of celebrating entities. The donkey represents the animal form worn by her Follower, and the fact that she is depicted as a youth is a sign that she has realized the meaning of this mystery. No longer trapped in the fearful and disconnected world of aging and death, she has found the "eternal youth" of the free soul itself, which is to say that she knows herself as a perpetual being created by the perpetual motion of the timeless system of co-creation and relationship. Her Fetch-Follower that she rides upon has helped her to reach this point; they are together in Interbeing.

Before them a Hobb walks, blowing his horn. Part human animal, part non-human animal, he is a symbol of the intimate relationship between humans and non-humans. Ahead of him, a red-haired woman with horns sprouting from her head stands. She was in her human life a witch of Scotland, but now, long after her death, she has crossed the division between the human experience and the other-than-human world, and the experience of Interbeing consciously fills her and completes her.

She is greeting a great black stag, for in her breathing life this was the form that the Master of witches and sorcerers (or perhaps one of his serving-daimons) took to teach her and her fellows. She meets him now, face to face again, a complete being like him. His promise of a great glory beyond the limited difficulties of her life is made good forever.

Beyond the parade of inter-relationship and wisdom, the great Hedge that once represented the division between unwise human beings and the massive reaches of the Unseen World is depicted, but it is now forever open with a green gateway. For those who have obtained the realization of this mystery, the division is no more. Never again will they stumble in the real darkness that is forgetfulness or unawareness of Interbeing.

The Sun card is the first of the cards that lacks "reversed" meanings in this system. It is always a card of sublime joy, realization, peace, and liberation. To have it appear reversed in any reading never really diminishes this; it merely gently reminds us to look towards the most fundamental fact of our existence – Interbeing – and to trust in the Fitness of Things, which is bright and real, no matter how dark perceptual situations in human life can get. A reversal indicates that we may be in a situation where we have forgotten this fact or can't feel it for the many reasons we often cannot.

XX: JUDGEMENT

XX: Judgment

As we proceeded through the cosmos represented by the twenty mysteries (remembering that the "zero" mystery, The Fool, and the final mystery, The World, stand apart, in a structural sense from cards I-XX) we were able to gain much insight through the pairing of the cards on the exoteric and esoteric sides of the Tarot schema. We were able to see, for instance, how Mystery III (The Empress) and Mystery XIII (Death) represented the fateful pairing of the womb and the tomb. Each of the ten pairs of mysteries formed this way tell an important story of the seen interacting with the unseen and vice-versa.

As we proceeded through the outward world, the more ordinarily expressed world represented by cards I-X, we reached the final card of that sequence – card X, The Wheel of the World, and saw that it represented the cycles of time and change that all who dwell in the ordinary world experience. In the same way that mystery XXI (The World) holds all of the other cards within herself, The Wheel of the World holds all of the exoteric mysteries of cards I-IX within itself. They play out, in their obvious and expressed way, within The Wheel of the World.

In mystery station XX, the station traditionally called "Judgement", we meet the mystery that is metaphysically paired with The Wheel of the World. While The Wheel of the World represents ordinary cycles of time and the perceptual experience of birth, growth, and death that is seemingly all-embracing, (alongside the seasons and the many other changeable forces that rule over the outwardly expressed cosmos) Judgement represents the reality of "extraordinary time" – or to put it more directly, timelessness.

In the deep heart of the world of changes lives a reality of timeless strangeness. It doesn't do to try and create some over-simple duality of "time" versus "timelessness" or "change" versus "changelessness." There is a tendency to want to do this, and many have done it, but the truth of the matter is more nuanced. The truth is also made more difficult to comprehend by the fact that some of these ordinary "duality" insights contain some accurate elements.

Mystery station XX, Judgement, does point towards the reality of eternity that lives within the wearisome turning of mortal time. It does point towards the idea of the "immortal hour" that is at the heart of all ordinary hours. But it's far more than just this. Judgement points to the existence of a land, a world, a place, or a condition of experience that is crucial to the cosmological system that Tarot works within.

In some sense, Judgement depicts the Unseen World as a whole, the mysterious Unseen that holds within itself all of the mysteries numbered XI-XIX, just as The Wheel of the World depicts the Seen World as a whole, holding within itself all of the mysteries numbered I through IX: But once again, the attempt to stop at this neat understanding causes a loss of something precious and subtle in the message here.

The surreal and powerful "dream-time" at the heart of ordinary time is itself *the origin* of our ability to perceive ordinary time. The Otherworld/Underworld that is at the heart of everything in the ordinary world is *the origin* of this ordinary world we experience. It's the origin of all beings, too.

These two things (the ordinary and the extraordinary), thought of as a simple duality, aren't standing across a chasm from each other; they are blended together, never able to be found apart. The "hedge" that separates ordinary human perceptions from the extraordinary perceptions of the unseen world is a hedge of exactly that – perception.

The barrier between our world and the extraordinary world has been depicted in many forms folklorically and mythologically (a wall, a river, etc.) But it's all the same idea. Here we must confront the idea that these things that seem very separate are very much enmeshed.

When the traveler faced the fearful things that needed to be faced in the stage of The Moon, and gained the transformative realization represented by The Sun, they didn't actually see a great sunrise over the dark realm of the moon. The dark realm of the moon is still the dark realm of the moon, and they were still right there inside it. What rose inside them was the light of realization. The light of The Sun in the esoteric mysteries is interior illumination. Filled with this illumination, this realization of the truth of their existence, the traveler was no longer afraid and no longer confused.

Having reached that point represented by The Sun, they were free. No illusion or fear of the Moon's realm could trap them within themselves. The entire infinity and timelessness of the Unseen World was as open, clear, and welcoming to them as any field or meadow in the ordinary world of their ordinary lives. Where the traveler goes from that point, or in what shape he goes, is entirely up to his mind and heart. It matters not where he goes, or if he even moves from that spot ever again; he is never lost or homeless.

He will, in all likelihood seek to help other beings; they are his kin, after all, and kin came from the common womb for one another. He now has the wisdom and subtle, far-seeing insight to help in the deepest possible ways. The "Underworld Initiation" is complete.

On our Tarot image, a man dressed in green has emerged from an ancient burial mound, a tomb-passage that leads to the Underworld. He's just back from the Underworld, come up from the darkness below and now walking under the bright light in a joyful world of springtime and new life. It is an image of regeneration, of rebirth. But it conceals a radically important mystery. For you must ask yourself "If seen and unseen are so thoroughly enmeshed, if time and timelessness are so hard to separate, what are you really seeing in this image?"

Is this a man who died, passed through the Underworld, and has finally taken rebirth as a new mortal, setting out (as The Fool did before) on another journey through The Wheel of the World? In other words, does that burial mound behind him, with its womb-like appearance and opening, represent the mother that just gave him a new mortal life? Is that the "front" of the womb-mound that he just emerged from? Are those flowers the flowers of our mortal world?

Or is this an image of a traveler who is coming out of the "back" of the mound? Is this the afterlife, the Underworld, the Unseen world that awaits all who have died? Has he died, passed through the grave represented by the burial mound and found himself in the Meadows of Elfhame, the home-country of the dead? Are those flowers the flowers of the Underworld?

Could this perhaps be an image of a realized person, whose experience of the dark Underworld has been transformed by the light of interior realization, and is now dwelling as a complete being in the "Pure Land", the timeless green world of Fayerie that has never fallen into the woes of mortal unwisdom?

In this image, you are seeing *all of these things at the same time*. It can represent any of them, for all are different forms of rebirth. For the ordinary person who lives and dies, life is a journey around The Wheel of the World and death is a passageway into the strange stages of the esoteric mysteries beyond, but that person has little power to consciously engage the mysteries. They wander from place to place, guided as much as they can be by the powers that accompany them and attempt to help them, before finally either assuming a new shape or existence in the Unseen or sometimes joining with the natural forces that bring persons back to ordinary life through the womb. They emerge into their new mortal life not able to remember much or understand the strangeness that came before.

The fundamental realization represented by The Sun is not fully had by them while in the ordinary world or the Unseen, and so they wander. Onward they are always going through many shapes and experiences. For that person, this card represents either dwelling in the deep as a postmortem Underworldly being, or coming back from the world beyond the grave through the womb of a mother and living in the ordinary world again.

But for the mystic or initiate who lives and dies, death brings them consciously from mystery stage to mystery stage, and to the fundamental realization. They may have had that realization in life, before they died, and they may have been very wise in the ordinary world because of it. However, death makes it complete; it makes their power and freedom as beings complete. They no longer wander under the compulsion of confusion; they wander under the delight of freedom. For that person, this card represents dwelling in the timelessness at the heart of all things, in the fullness of being.

And their condition is depicted as an eternal beautiful world of ageless youth, a world beyond the tired back-and-forth of life, aging and death. This is the Fayerie world that mortals sometimes, in the old stories, find themselves caught away to, or kidnapped and taken to – a world where time passes very differently from the mortal world. A day there can be years in the ordinary world. Some of the beings who dwell there are fearful, dangerous, or still living out different styles of confusion, just like the beings in the ordinary world. Some are wise and realized beings, just as some beings are in the ordinary world.

The man in our image is True Thomas, also called Thomas the Rhymer, "all kilted in green" – a sign that he has passed through the Underworld or Fayerie-land and merged with the depths the green world. He has emerged transformed into a complete being by it. Green is a traditional color of death in folkloric terms because to be dead is to be within the land, below the greenery.

Thomas was a man who lived in 13th century Scotland and who obtained his initiation through an encounter with the Queen of the Fayerie people. He dwelled with those powers, learning from them for seven years in the Underworld. Like all who gain the fundamental mystery-realization that leads to the ultimate depths of wisdom, Thomas didn't do it alone. He was helped by the Fayerie Queen and other powers. All who come successfully through the esoteric mysteries have help and must have help.

Upon his return, he had the power of prophecy, among other powers. Having gone beyond life and death, he still lives as a powerful being with a quality of living presence that can (and does) still impact the ordinary world of our experience today. He can, and sometimes does, appear to ordinary people in dreams and visions. If he chose to, he could assume a more obvious form (just as you or I possess) and interact in a more ordinary way.

For realized beings can do that. They are no longer trapped by any confusions, and no longer limited in power as we understand it. They can, from the timeless felicity in which they dwell, manipulate the subtle powers to appear in the dreams of mortals, or appear as phantoms or visions. They can join with the forces of life to find the allies needed to assume a mortal shape, and live as we do, but without any forgetfulness of their true beings and with none of the confusion we live under. It is all within the realm of possibility for them. They are the "Justified Ones", the Truly Wise. They can dwell in the world we see ordinarily or in the world unseen, or both, as they choose. From our perspective, they can be anywhere or nowhere at all.

Thomas' walking staff in our image is a three-tined staff, representing the path he took to find his way into the Fayerie-Queen's realm, where his merging and initiation took place. He faced a choice, as all of the people who come to the Underworld do, of going left or right at a crossroads. To go right would have meant choosing a thoughtless, ordinary life of obscurity and forgetfulness. To go left would have meant choosing an extraordinary life of personal sacrifice and pain that would help many.

He chose neither. The Fayerie Queen gave him the power to see a hidden third way that took him to Her realm.

He took the hidden mean between the extremes of duality that trap most mortals, the excluded center that leads to wisdom.

The image of this card asks us to do the same, if we wish to see it for what it is. It isn't either an image of a dead and reborn ordinary person starting a new life, or an image of a realized person dwelling in the timeless condition. It's something between them. It's both, in one sense, but also a special realization that binds the two. The people we meet in this world – are they living or dead? The people or beings we might meet in the Underworld – are they alive or dead?

In the sky above this Thomas, who might be freshly back from the Underworld of Fayerie, or who might just be wandering around in those Fayerie-meadows enjoying himself, a fiery orb burns in the sky, containing an image of the Master of the Wild Hunt. He is the leader of the spirit-host that calls to death all of the living whose time has come to undergo the change of death. He's blowing his horn that calls souls out of their enmeshment in ordinary life and which makes the terrifying sound of fateful inevitability.

The fire that surrounds the Master of Life and Death is the fire of the timeless, which burns up time-bound mortal perceptions, revealing deeper, stranger truths. Worlds and lives both end in this fire and are reborn from it, too.

The mythical dimension of life has been fully realized and actualized by the person-principle at this stage. This is the culmination and completion of all mysteries.

XXI: THE WORLD

XXI: The World

Each of the mysteries from Arcanum I (The Sorcerer) to Arcanum XX (Judgement) are distinct mystery-systems, or mystery-ecologies, which means that they refer not just to events, insights, and natural realities but also to families of power – to actual groupings of persons and entities.

The Sorcerer card refers to the family of entities that indwell the winds of this world and the Great Indweller of the Wind Himself (to make an example.) This a the family of entities that teach sorcery and cunning, and bestow ordinary and extraordinary forms of reason and intellectual strength. Human sorcerers and sorceresses are included in this family, on its esoteric side; but on a more exoteric side, stage magicians, con-men, and even scientists, architects, or craftsmen might be thought to be related to it. For it is a station involved with the intellect and the intellect's way of measuring and manipulating the world.

The Empress card, to continue this explanation, refers to the family of entities that bestow fertility and accompany the coming-to-being of life in the sensual world. It also includes the powers of the fertility of the land, and the Great Indweller in the Earth Herself. It would also include human mothers or non-human mothers, and people who manifest the Venusian aspect of sensual life, like sex workers or anyone involved deeply in the sensual grace of life.

The Death card encapsulates the powers that govern the dying process. The Strength card refers to the class of entities we have called "Followers" or familiar spirits and fetches. The Devil card refers to the Hobbs, the wild entities beyond the boundaries of civilization who bestow initiations upon sorcerers and witches. It also includes the Master-spirit as the Wild Hunter and Chthonic Lord of Spirits. This list of examples could go on almost endlessly for each card.

For the sake of being able to have a "system" of esoteric understanding at all, it was needful for the Tarot system to reduce things down to twenty major groupings of powers. In reality, there might be countless. The fundamental powers most obvious to human experience were categorized into the twenty mysteries, and from that point, people can extrapolate from within them the many layers of subtlety that must be involved.

The final card in the Greater Arcana sequence, card XXI, The World, is the numerical culmination of the sequence and the image of the World that holds within itself all of the mysteries that came before. The World is the stage upon which the twenty previous powers play themselves out in interaction with one another. The World is the great landscape, with its seen and unseen realms, that The Fool moves through as he journeys along and discovers things, perhaps becoming wise in the long run.

The World's image is the all-inclusive image of the supreme message of the Tarot Mysteries. It shows a woman – The Feminine Spirit of the World (a form of the Earth Indweller, the All-Mother) naked and opening Her arms, giving all and receiving all. Around Her coils the Red Serpent which is (as we have seen) the primordial form of the Master of Life Himself. The undifferentiated power of life-force in Him finds, through Her womb, a way to assume endless particulate forms of life. Together, these two great beings merge to symbolize the rapture of life itself, the great animating force of The World.

To symbolize the inexhaustible power of this great co-creation, the Feminine Spirit of the World stands in a yonic-shaped space. Above Her head is a sigil that gives access to the Underworld or to the Unseen, access to the source of things. Below Her feet is the three-pronged "Elfhame Cross" which we first saw in Thomas the Rhymer's walking-staff in Card XX, and it carries the same meaning.

Around these two figures and their fertile space is foliage from all four seasons and four beasts that represent the essence of those seasons. The plants and animals being depicted here alongside the human shape at the center say that the same essence of life manifests and fills all these forms. The seasonal motif suggests a hint of The Wheel of the World; all these lives dwell within the cycles of living and dying and being reborn. Everything is here. Everything is related, whether they are beasts of air, earth, or water. This is an image of completeness, of The Fitness of Things, of Interbeing, and of the deepest and most profound possible Good. It says "All is Well."

The female figure in the center also represents the realized initiate, whether male or female. In our image it is a red-haired woman, a reference to the red-haired Scottish witch depicted on card XIX, but it could refer to any person who has obtained the illumination of wisdom and now dances open and rapturously amid the forces of life. It represents all who are now eternally liberated and able to be just what they are without shame, confusion, or guilt. The truth at the heart of things has set them free.

In much the same way that The World itself contains the spaces in which the mysteries and the many communities of life play out their endless game of interaction, the body and soul of the initiate is another kind of world. It is a living microcosm in which the mysteries they encounter, experience, and internalize in life and death play themselves out, too.

The four creatures and the four seasonal stations that surround the Feminine World Spirit also connect to the idea of the "four elements" – the traditional esoteric elements (Earth, Air, Fire, and Water) that give rise to the world in a very tangible, material sense. They also give rise to the four suits of Minor Arcana cards that belong to traditional Tarot decks as well. Thus, The World Card doesn't just hold the entirety of the Major Arcana inside Herself, She also holds the Minor Arcana's elemental court cards and pip cards inside Herself too.

Those four elemental suits of the Minor Arcana flow from the four corners of The World Card, if you wish to see it that way. The Goat represents Spring and fire and the suit of staves; the Stag represents Summer and earth and the suit of coins, the Toad represents Autumn and water and the suit of cups, and the Owl represents Winter and air and the suit of swords. These four broad groupings of associations also make reference to the will (Goat), the body (Stag), the free soul (Toad) and the breath soul (Owl.) Many other beasts could have been chosen to make these traditional representations; these were chosen for personal reasons on the part of this writer.

The World card is the symbol of the deepest and best good, The Fitness of All Things, and is the second and last card in the Tarot system that has no "reversed" position nor reversed meanings. It is always a positive card, always a sign of goodness in abundance, of good things to come, or of a person being somewhere they are meant to be and doing things they are meant to do.

It is important to note that the mystery-sequence itself culminates in experience and meaning with Card XX, Judgement. Card XXI, The World, is (like The Fool) one of the two cards that stands outside the sequence of twenty cards but still maintains a deep, intrinsic relationship to all of them.

II:

The Suggested Card Meanings for Readings

0: The Fool

Upright: Carefree

<u>General:</u> Wisdom, Clear seeing, creativity, spontaneity, a new beginning, light heartedness. Can mean carelessness, but not in some overly harmful way, at least on the surface.

<u>State of Mind or Soul:</u> Overflowing eagerness or excitement when realizing the potentials of life, the mind, or the soul. Basic happiness or enjoyment, always somewhat naïve. A state of simplicity, but not in any pejorative sense of that word.

<u>Relational:</u> The feeling of "crush", new relationship bliss, flirting, enjoyment with partner(s), happiness. Non-traditional relationship styles.

<u>Employment:</u> Creative breakthrough, clean slates, new ideas that inspire, admirable skill due to being fresh-minded.

Reversed: Foolish

<u>General:</u> Foolishness, not seeing what is necessary or important, mistakes, irresponsibility, dangerous carelessness.

<u>State of Mind or Soul:</u> limited perceptions/narrow mindedness, self-centeredness, chaos or confusion. A heavy heart. Feeling quite unable to move freely or being burdened.

<u>Relational:</u> Neglecting partner(s), not being sensitive to others, or careless with feelings. Selfishness that one may not even realize they are projecting.

<u>Employment:</u> Neglecting important duties, not wanting to be open to new things, lack of experience. Clumsy errors. Sloppiness.

I: The Sorcerer

Upright: Skillful

General: Skillfulness, charisma, intelligence, wit, confidence, vitality and energy. Persuasion and persuasiveness, even manipulation, but not in a harmful way. Being a good performer or communicator.

State of Mind or Soul: Great clarity for the world, being able to make sense of things satisfyingly. The desire to assert oneself, to figure things out, to make a name for oneself or excel. Feeling capable or confident. A keen desire to figure things out. The hidden desire to impress others or prove oneself.

Relational: Being fair with others, skillfully integrating self with others, shaping things with charm or subtlety to everyone's satisfaction. Oaths and agreements intelligently made and kept.

Employment: Being an exemplar of skill at a craft, a creative and shining star within a craft or field, mastering tasks, success, hard work, achievements of art.

Reversed: Deceitful

<u>General:</u> Deceit and manipulation in the harmful sense, confidence trick, use of personal skill for dark or ruthless ends. Not respecting others or seeing others as means to ends. Callousness. Taking advantage of others, or being taken advantage of.

<u>State of Mind or Soul:</u> Becoming enmeshed in lies and deceits, reacting to things without regard for the truth or what may be best for self or others. Feeling defensive and willing to manipulate others to protect oneself. Feeling resentful or jealous of those that you perceive to be competitors.

<u>Relational:</u> Lies and manipulations between friends or partners. One side of a relationship kept in the dark. People being used. Unpredictable behavior between friends or partners.

<u>Employment:</u> The theft of other's work or efforts, work based on falsehoods, false acclaim, using others for personal gain, succeeding through unscrupulous means. Feeling unable to trust others.

II: The Sorceress

Upright: Mysterious

<u>General:</u> Strange feelings or encounters that benefit a person, leading to wisdom. Intuition. Dreams. Mystical visions that bestow guidance. The presence of the dead, or spirits, or unknown powers who influence things, generally in positive or ambiguous ways. The urgings of the soul. Seership.

<u>State of Mind or Soul:</u> Being in the grip of strange, mystical, or surreal experiences. Being guided. Knowing deeper truths. Desire or passion for the unseen and the strange or occult things. Artistic inspiration.

<u>Relational:</u> Feeling deeply connected to a partner or to others. A felt sense of destiny between people, or a "deeper reason" for their meeting or relating. Mutual bonds and trust. Enjoying moments together that only those who were there would understand.

<u>Employment:</u> Artistic inspiration, therapeutic or spiritual work, good instincts for a task or a job, things "working out" in some strange or unexpected (but ultimately happy) way.

Reversed: Unpredictable

General: Disturbing visions or bizarre, chaotic experiences that confuse. Being cut off from intuition or ignoring intuition and feelings. Strange things occurring that make one feel helpless and anxious. Loss of guidance. Hidden powers working in ways that one didn't expect or desire.

State of Mind or Soul: Feeling disconnected from anything except the shallow surface of things. Feeling that things are banal or pointless. Feeling threatened by forces one can't understand. Yearning for inspiration or clarity that seems out of reach.

Relational: Forgetting the depth of one's bonds with others. Losing positive regard for others. Untrustworthy behavior between persons. Disappointments with others, even if it is unfair to be disappointed.

Employment: Being uninspired and forcing oneself to make efforts. Things feeling (and perhaps actually being) out of control and not worth effort.

III: The Empress

Upright: Pleasurable

General: Pleasure, sensuality, natural happiness, fertility, pregnancy and birth, health, allure and attraction. Powerful or healthy growth. Generosity.

State of Mind or Soul: Feeling happy, calm, or at peace (as when one has a potent experience of beauty or nature), feeling energetic or optimistic about life or oneself, feeling productive. Feeling well-disposed to join with others on many levels. The desire to find companionship or create.

Relational: Great, mutually-enjoyable sensuality between partners. "Honeymoon." Being deeply in love. Wanting to pleasure other people, or show devotion, care, or love.

Employment: Growing opportunities, growing skill, great output, happiness in work. Great new ideas or efforts. Originality.

Reversed: Sterile

<u>General:</u> Sterility, the lack of growth or the loss of something vital and beautiful. Depression. Slowing down. Withering. Inability to find much enjoyment in things. Illness. Exploitation or degeneracy of emotions. Stinginess. Pollution or desecration of the natural world. Illness or disease.

<u>State of Mind or Soul:</u> Depression, anhedonia, or self loathing. Feeling repelled or repulsed by others.

<u>Relational:</u> Having little or no feelings or desires for partner(s). Emotional cool-down between people. Perhaps the desire to break away from others or leave a partner or partners.

<u>Employment:</u> Inability to produce or make many efforts. Poor "harvest" of output or gains. Lack of enthusiasm. Mass production that lacks any real inspiration or spirit.

IV: The Emperor

Upright: Authoritative

<u>General:</u> Strong will, or the activity of the will, but with a sense of moderation and skill. Fair judgments. Acquisitions without acrimony or harm to others. Sense of responsibility and good leadership. Realism, pragmatism. Initiative and strength. Institutions of government and military authority.

<u>State of Mind or Soul:</u> Delight in structure and order, sometimes too much so. A feeling of security or predictability for one's surroundings and for others. The urge to assert one's will and create control over forces or the environment around oneself.

<u>Relational:</u> Secure foundations for partnerships, good working together, goals mutually being realized, an experienced relationship that may have endured tests before.

<u>Employment:</u> Leadership in profession, promotion, perfectionism, becoming influential, realizing goals.

Reversed: Tyrannical

<u>General:</u> Tyranny. Using strength and even violence to obtain things no matter the costs to others. Love of authority, and overlooking the excesses, contradictions, or cruelty required by authority. Brutality and control. War. Fascism. Nationalism.

<u>State of Mind or Soul:</u> Arrogant disregard for others. A fear of the world or others that triggers anger or hate and a desire to control things violently. Prideful egomania. Feeling threatened by other beings or forces.

<u>Relational:</u> Abuse of others within a relationship. Non-mutual relationship realities which give gains to one, but detriment to the other(s). Grotesque power games. Fear or resentment between people.

<u>Employment:</u> A bad boss who abuses workers, a toxic workplace or environment, bullies and dark power games that inhibit work, cooperation or creativity, a bad leader, waste. Forces that constrain enjoyment or production.

V: The Pope

Upright: Conformity

General: Transmission of teachings, information, and learning. Teaching. Social conditioning. Education. Trust. Conformity. A good teacher or knowledgeable professor or source of knowledge. The mainstream of a society or the social world. Institutions of educational and spiritual authority. Faith in mainstream beliefs. Idealism. Lesson.

State of Mind or Soul: The feeling of delight in conformity. Feeling connected to those around you, and the feeling of belonging to a group. Willingness to learn, to be taught. Trusting in the unseen. The desire to find one's place. Can imply a certain limitation on imagination.

Relational: Traditional relationships, trust between partners, one partner learning much from the other, learning from one another, finding meaning in relationships. Stable relationships.

Employment: Following a calling, being a trusted person or advisor, gaining good counsel, educating oneself about one's craft or profession, expanding one's understanding, or teaching others. Gaining mainstream recognition. Stability.

Reversed: Rigidity

<u>General:</u> Over-conformity and rigidity, fraud, manipulation, spiritual or cultural elitism or imperialism, being judgmental and dismissive to others, taking advantage of others of weaker mind or will, paranoia, "cult leader." Hypocrisy.

<u>State of Mind or Soul:</u> Closed-minded arrogance or ignorance. The desire to see contrary positions or ideas silenced or made invisible. Refusing better perspectives and their potentials, and holding on doggedly to previous ideas, even flawed ones. Major deficit of imagination.

<u>Relational:</u> Using shame or guilt to control or influence a partner or partners. Shame or guilt between the partners. Inability for partners to open their minds to each other's differing perspectives. Double standards.

<u>Employment:</u> Relying on the letter of the law, but not the spirit of the law. Being uncompromising, rejecting new learning or insights. Inflexibility with one's profession or craft. Over-reliance on outside authorities.

VI: The Lovers

Upright: Attraction and Co-Creation

<u>General:</u> Attraction, the urge to union, lust, desire, romance, and co-creation. Overcoming obstacles or differences. Fruitful friendship or alliance. Courting. Marriage.

<u>State of Mind or Soul:</u> Realizing what things naturally or fruitfully belong together, enjoyment of pleasure, feelings of loving devotion. The urge to find love and realize great things, or to find one's destiny or purpose.

<u>Relational:</u> The bliss of lovers, happy marriages, good alliances that yield good things, the wildness of "crush", satisfaction with others.

<u>Employment:</u> Joining resources or powers with others to get things done, enjoying one's work or vocation, compromises, excellent teamwork. Feeling connected to an institution, field, place, or vocation.

Reversed: Obsession

<u>General:</u> Possessiveness, obsession, the desire to take others (persons or otherwise) even against their will or against what is rightful, co-dependency. Jealousy. Insecurity.

<u>State of Mind or Soul:</u> The desire to control others or force them to feel or act a certain way. Being unable to think or act outside of emotional drives. Belief that one can force love or emotions to be a certain way.

<u>Relational:</u> Overbearing situation between partners or friends. Relationships that continue out of habit, despite no longer being healthy or fruitful. Jealous games.

<u>Employment:</u> Refusing to join with others even though it would be beneficial, not feeling inspired, being uncompromising or against teamwork. Workaholic with the element of perfectionism.

VII: The Chariot

Upright: Progress

<u>General:</u> Movement, progress, motion, advancement. One's path through life, and often as it carries one to Fateful and needful places wherein and whereby growth happens. Competition and challenge, often to success. Making a great leap forward. Being supported by fortunate, hidden powers.

<u>State of Mind or Soul:</u> Feeling as though one is following the path one is intended to follow. Confidence. Feeling energetic and able to face challenges. The urge to charge and fight. The urge to achieve.

<u>Relational:</u> Making good progress in relationships, to the benefit of all involved. Sometimes a new relationship is forecast. Helping one another, making efforts together.

<u>Employment:</u> Advancement of career or skill. Self-employment. Starting a new project or finishing old ones and reaping good rewards. A lucky turn that allows for growth.

Reversed: Delay or Halt

<u>General:</u> Delay, halt, comedy of errors, distraction, wrong turn. Failure to make progress, or circumstances that bring a person to a painful or limited place. Lack of achievement or a failure to express oneself in a satisfying way. Failure of plans or failure to meet goals.

<u>State of Mind or Soul:</u> Feeling hopeless or stuck. Feeling unable to change one's circumstances for the better. Feeling lost. The urge to rebel or revolt. Anger and frustration.

<u>Relational:</u> A relationship that has stagnated, and ceased to produce growth or good changes for people involved. A dead-end relationship or alliances. Boredom with others. Feeling alienated from others.

<u>Employment:</u> Demotion or lack of advancement at work or on projects. Writer's block. Tedium. Inability to feel energetic about tasks. Inability to bring things together or to decide where to go.

VIII: Justice

Upright: Fair Returns

<u>General:</u> Fair returns. Natural balance. Fairness. Consequences, but not always overly harsh ones. Being tested and found worthy. Wise avoidance of troubles or conflicts. Things being moderate, or embracing wise moderation. Not straying from the path. Can mean harsh but deserved or logical consequences.

<u>State of Mind or Soul:</u> Recognizing that Nature has her own inescapable binding laws and that your own existence (and everything else) fits into them. Knowing one's place in a larger sense. Feeling justified. Atonement. Having worldly wisdom for consequences and the way things work. Accepting one's just deserts.

<u>Relational:</u> A balanced love or relational life with others, people being fair with one another, giving other people space and respect.

<u>Employment:</u> Fair contracts, balanced books, professionalism, fair treatment of partners or clients or others, gaining the returns and rewards that one has honestly worked for.

Reversed: Imbalance

<u>General:</u> Unfairness, imbalance, lack of fair reciprocity. Corruption, injustice, bias, prejudice, and wasteful greed or waste generally. Trespass. Violations of decency. Destruction of life. A desire for vengeance is created.

<u>State of Mind or Soul:</u> Paranoia, guilt, fear. The urge to struggle against nature or things that can't be changed. Living unaware of what is truly good or bad, helpful or harmful.

<u>Relational:</u> People in a relationship being taken bad advantage of. Oppressed people, or oppressive behaviors. Using people up and discarding them.

<u>Employment:</u> Not getting fair return for good or honest labors. Exploitation.

IX: The Hermit

Upright: Mature Introspection

General: Conviction, personal strength, wealth of experience. Introspection. Contemplation and gaining insight, the calm maturity of age or the maturity gained through hardships. Steadiness, slowness, sometimes patience. A sage or wise person. Someone no longer trapped by social fictions, but may be disillusioned in ways. Memory. Nostalgia. Regrets. Gaining clarity or defining oneself. The limit of something. The horizon of something. Courage. Boundary. Horizon. Solitary pursuits or solitary life.

State of Mind or Soul: Feeling secure within oneself, and with oneself. Coming into one's own, mentally and emotionally. Submitting to larger life-forces and learning from them. Deep honesty with oneself. Wanting to help others on account of personal experience. Reaching the limit of one's understanding about a matter.

Relational: Mature relationships, mature dealings between people, patience between people, being true to oneself and resisting bad compromises. Sometimes means temporary separations or retreats to allow people time to consider things. Can also refer to the choice to be single.

Employment: Training others, being the experienced one people come to, passing experience onto others, retreating from a job or craft for a while or for good, changing careers or crafts to be more in line with who you've become.

Reversed: Resignation

<u>General:</u> Resignation. Cynicism, bitterness, and lack of insight. Nihilistic thinking or despair. A person who has given up or a situation that seems beyond anyone's reach or repair. Lack of convictions, bad experiences that didn't give birth to wisdom, but to cruelty or coldness. Ignoring the past. An unwise person or idea. Mental or emotional immaturity. Denial of hard truths. Fear or change or fear generally. Fear of others, recluse.

<u>State of Mind or Soul:</u> Feeling insecure and being in denial about one's past or weaknesses within oneself. Being cynical and dismissive of others. Overestimating oneself or pridefully looking down on others.

<u>Relational:</u> Pushing others away, taking things out on others, cold behavior. Forcing people into bad compromises, giving bad advice, or being unconcerned for others generally.

<u>Employment:</u> Performing a task or craft or job one hates, being cold to other people around one in a profession or craft, dissatisfaction with a job or craft. Passing on bad skills or examples or ethics. Burnout.

X: The Wheel of the World

Upright: Good Development

General: Time passing. Optimism. Energy. Circumstances in motion, but changing for the better. An up-turn in fortune. Repetition. Changes. Larger, Fateful powers showing their influence.

State of Mind or Soul: Seeing oneself and one's life as a small part of a larger thing, particularly a large and complex world. Humbleness, but not in any unhealthy way. Hope for things becoming better. Accepting one's place. Natural enjoyment of the world, for all its blessings and difficulties.

Relational: Happy turns or changes in a relationship. Seeing bigger relationship patterns. Feeling like one can be with another or in a relationship to others for a long time. Fateful encounters.

Employment: Fulfilling one's vocation, realizing one's calling, being very satisfied by what one does. Good fortune in professional matters.

Reversed: Ill Circumstances

<u>General:</u> Painful passage of time. Pessimism. Weariness. Circumstances in motion, but changing for ill. A down-turn in fortune. Impatience. Hardships. Being overwhelmed by forces outside of one's control.

<u>State of Mind or Soul:</u> Thinking that one is the "center of the world" and the inflation of ego that follows. Ignoring the larger realities of the world in favor of petty concerns. Despair over things ever getting better. Hating the world or ignoring it by taking shelter in imaginary ideas of transcendence.

<u>Relational:</u> The slow diminishing of a relationship, or disillusionment over time with a partner or partners. Inability to see the patterns that bind one's relationship(s). Feeling like a relationship won't last.

<u>Employment:</u> Working steadily, but not feeling as though one is living up to one's potential. Feeling despair of ever finding one's dream job or real task in life. Bad fortune in professional matters, or a down-turn in professional performance or options.

XI: Strength

Upright: Help Received

General: Strength of will or interior strength and confidence. Spiritual power. A trustworthy ally. Deep connections that allow a person to succeed or find strength. Passion. Connection. Extraordinary resources that can be drawn upon. Guidance. Protection.

State of Mind or Soul: The ecstasy of discovering deep truths within oneself. The bliss that accompanies knowledge of one's soul, or self-knowledge that makes one stronger. The feeling of confidence that comes from good allies or friends. Feeling strong.

Relational: Powerful, passionate connection with another person or persons. Shared happiness. Mutual protection and aid.

Employment: Great motivation and certainty of one's power to achieve. Excellent teamwork or teammates. Achievement. Overcoming difficulties.

Reversed: Vulnerability

<u>General:</u> Vulnerability. Exposed. Weak will. Feeling little connection to subtle matters. Doubts and denials. Feeling as though one has no real friends or trustworthy ones. Feeling alone or vulnerable. Weakness.

<u>State of Mind or Soul:</u> Feeling alienated from others and sensing no meaning below the surface of things. World weariness. Isolated pain. Feeling weak.

<u>Relational:</u> Unrequited feelings between people. Insincerity. Divided goals and plans. Failure to give or receive help when it is needed.

<u>Employment:</u> Doubts about one's ability to succeed or achieve. One's ability to succeed or achieve hampered by obstacles seen and unseen. Little or no support for one's projects or goals.

XII: The Hanged Man

Upright: Painful Transition

General: Agony. Crisis. Being crucified or suspended between painful choices. Being stuck or helpless or immobilized. Pain and suffering that still yields potentially good or potent transformations. Martyrdom. Facing the unknown. Trapped.

State of Mind or Soul: Feeling helpless and frightened. The sense of dread and the inevitable. Feeling committed to a course of action, even if it is difficult or costly. Self Sacrifice.

Relational: A situation that cannot be resolved without someone in a partnership or group getting hurt. Feeling stuck in a relationship with no easy way out. Complicated situations without easy solutions, or with no good solutions. Rocky relationships that have a high potential of ending.

Employment: Inability to find work or employment. Working hard to no avail. Desperation to succeed. Work stress of a high degree.

Reversed: Ruin

<u>General:</u> Ruin. Great suffering, but without the potential to yield any positive transformations. Being broken by suffering. Grave injustice or error. Great loss. Becoming a scapegoat or targeted by a lynch mob. Masochism. Victim.

<u>State of Mind or Soul:</u> Broken-mindedness or lost grip on reality. Inability to cope. Personality change, but not in a positive way. Inability to speak for oneself or act in one's best interests.

<u>Relational:</u> Suffering endlessly for others, without receiving help in return or appreciation. Being the target for others to take out frustrations. Lack of respect between people. Loss of a relationship almost certainly.

<u>Employment:</u> Being fired or penalized unfairly. Being unable to change one's work or craft situation for the better. Inability to make any progress.

XIII: Death

Upright: Change

<u>General:</u> Major but natural changes that are beyond one's control. Letting go of something. The need to let go. The end of something. Forced goodbyes. Missing others. Hardship. Adjustment.

<u>State of Mind or Soul:</u> Realizing how transient all things are, and being very appreciative of what you have while you have it. The ability to cope with changes.

<u>Relational:</u> End of a partnership or a relationship between people, a very large or fundamental change in the relationship for good or for ill, being parted from others, fear of losing a relationship.

<u>Employment:</u> Retirement. Being unable to keep up with changes in a field. Finishing great tasks. losing one's sense of connection to a task or craft or profession, or enthusiasm for it.

Reversed: Denial

<u>General:</u> Denial. Hard changes that one cannot avoid, which, though seemingly natural, are cruel or painful. Sorrow. Mourning. Being forced to let go of too much at once. Suddenly being parted from loved ones. Sudden loss of something treasured. The inability to let go.

<u>State of Mind or Soul:</u> Reacting fearfully or angrily against change by denying its power or existence. Creating rationalizations for why one need not let go when it is called for. Denial about hard things generally. Being lost in sorrow or bitter.

<u>Relational:</u> Being unable to accept that a relationship has ended, or move past it. Sorrow. Heartbreak. Depression.

<u>Employment:</u> Being suddenly dismissed or fired for reasons beyond your control. Having one's connection to a craft or profession severed or destroyed for some reason, or one's ability to engage it. Refusing to change when you see that the world is changing how your profession or craft operates, refusal to "stay current."

XIV: Temperance

Upright: Balancing

<u>General:</u> Balance, healing, proper or good proportions, finding peace after hardship, restoring harmony, a state of harmony or ease. Being inspired or protected by kindly powers beyond oneself. Union with helpful forces or persons. Receiving.

<u>State of Mind or Soul:</u> Feeling healed or released from a long-held stress or difficulty. Relief. Mental or spiritual tensions banished and replaced with true resolution.

<u>Relational:</u> Sexual or tantric alchemy between mates, passionate and mystically transformative exchanges between partners or friends, working very well together, balancing the needs of everyone in very helpful and healthy ways. Admiration or adoration for one another or others.

<u>Employment:</u> Overcoming problems or blockages in work or craft, or in a workplace; finding the good balance between work and recreation, or between seriousness and playfulness. Fruitful teamwork, excellent meetings between persons in pursuit of various goals.

Reversed: Anxiety

<u>General:</u> Anxiety, imbalance, ill proportions, inability to overcome contradictions or difficulties. Lack of harmony inside and outside of a person. Feeling vulnerable or lacking support. Loss.

<u>State of Mind or Soul:</u> Loneliness or feeling like no one understands or supports a person when things are hard. Chronic fear or anxiety. Inability to overcome quandaries in one's mind or soul, disquiet.

<u>Relational:</u> Shallow exchanges between partners or friends, meaningless movements or motions that don't bring people closer together in any authentic or deep way. People's needs not balanced against the needs of others.

<u>Employment:</u> Working to overcome problems or difficulties that continue to multiply or resist getting solved. Inability to really connect with others, to get help or guide everyone to mutual benefit. Inability to find needed help or support.

XV: The Devil

Upright: Wildness

<u>General:</u> A hardship that binds, but tends to lead to a greater freedom or insight in the long-term. Instincts and strange impulses. Wildness. Intoxication. Non-conformity. Strong emotions that make others uncomfortable. Unconscious powers. Strange or bizarre behavior or occurrences. Breaking free from long-held social restrictions or taboos, for good or for ill. Unexpected behaviors or changes.

<u>State of Mind or Soul:</u> Perceiving the wild, socially unacceptable aspect of the self. Being possessed by that "shadow" self. Being bold and uncaring about one's social environment or its expectations. Feeling rebellious or tired of dealing with the stresses and duties of the social world.

<u>Relational:</u> Bondage or binding to other people, for fateful or hard to understand reasons. Strange powers that bring people together or keep them together, like love sorcery. Conflicted relationships that still endure. Accepting the hard or uncomfortable things about others. Obsessions.

<u>Employment:</u> Unconventional methods or behaviors, which can be seen as brilliant or hard to work with. Playing "fast and loose" with rules and regulations. Intrigues. Illegal or semi-legal "dark dealings." Ambiguous relationships and methods.

Reversed: Malformation

<u>General:</u> Addiction. Abuse or pain. Slavery. Strong emotions or mental states that make a person unable to live in the ordinary world safely or successfully. Madness. Schizophrenia. Inability to communicate or be understood. Law-breaking and criminal behavior. Harmful mutation.

<u>State of Mind or Soul:</u> Feeling alien or unable to relate to others. Being obsessed by passions or activities that are far beyond acceptable to the social world. Dark secrets or joys that one cannot share, and which may exert a negative impact on exterior or interior life.

<u>Relational:</u> A mutually unhealthy relationship between partners or friends. Helping one another to come to harm. Being wild together, but using up each other's minds or souls in so doing. Relationships that can never be understood by outsiders or through any rational means. Downward spirals.

<u>Employment:</u> Rule-breaking and damaging behaviors in the pursuit of crafts or profits. Intimidating or manipulating others for dark ends. Being unable to produce anything that others would understand or value. Webs of lies that have gotten too thick to escape. Collapse of efforts.

XVI: The Ruined Tower

Upright: Repulsion and Division

<u>General:</u> Upheaval, Destruction, Separation, Massive revision, Extreme changes, Sudden news that shakes things up or shakes a person to their foundations, a breakthrough, liberation, the pain of having to pay for mistreatment to others. Fate's hard hand striking and changing something, usually out of necessity or for good in the long run. Conflict. Loss.

<u>State of Mind or Soul:</u> Giving up on long-held ideas or beliefs. Feeling one's deep-seated beliefs under siege or questioning them, and knowing that one can never go back to being or believing as they did before. Having one's mind expanded to new dimensions, often painfully.

<u>Relational:</u> A fast or unexpected separation, anger, fights, shouting, or resentfulness that severs bonds between people, the rocky relationship that gets harder and harder to hold together. The end of a relationship, a divorce or separation, usually not amicable. Major challenge to relationship.

<u>Employment:</u> Being fired or failing. Bankruptcy, lost property or resources, an unexpected change that destroys all of one's plans or hopes/dreams invested in the profession or craft. Total new beginning in a new field.

Reversed: Wanton Destruction

<u>General:</u> Savage violence or destruction that only leads to more misery. A breakthrough or insight that leads not to liberation, but to a new style of imprisonment. Hate. Extreme anger. Ruin. Super-egoism.

<u>State of Mind or Soul:</u> the mind warped by extreme hate or anger, making it difficult or impossible for a person to gain or keep close allies, or have much spiritual support or lasting insight. A toxic state of resentfulness and hatred that leads one to think of the world in dark terms. A mind broken by traumas or painful experiences from the past. Defeat.

<u>Relational:</u> The destruction or dissolution of relationships. Acrimonious endings of partnerships or relationships, or the inability to make or keep relationships at all. Extreme relationship stress.

<u>Employment:</u> loss of profession, reputation, or ability to work. Chronic unemployment. Scandals and ruin. Desperation, trying to make ends meet by woeful or tragic means.

XVII: The Star

Upright: Hopeful Rejuvenation

<u>General:</u> Hope, good chances, good prospects, peace, rest, guidance from greater or deeper forces, deep insight, sublime experiences, surreal and beautiful visions. Regeneration.

<u>State of Mind or Soul:</u> Learning to trust in the larger picture that you can't see. Peace. Feeling faith or hope for the future, even when things are very hard. Optimism.

<u>Relational:</u> A very inspiring love, benevolent bonds based on genuine selflessness, promising plans for the future between two people or a group of people, hopeful feelings about living together or being together or things done together.

<u>Employment:</u> Having excellent mentorship, promising opportunities or hopeful events showing a good way ahead, being safe from stresses or overwork, finding a new course for one's craft or profession that makes a person feel inspired and excited.

Reversed: Despair

<u>General:</u> Despair, bad chances, bad prospects, disquiet or disturbance, stress, feeling lost or unsure, hard experiences, exhaustion.

<u>State of Mind or Soul:</u> Refusal or inability to believe that deeper powers operate in the background and influence things. Feeling like the future is a lost cause. Pessimism. Being hard-hearted or jaded. Sadness or longing.

<u>Relational:</u> A very banal kind of connection that is still based on one-sided personal interest. No real plans for the future. Activities that are barely adequate to maintain bonds. Worry or pessimism over living together or relating together.

<u>Employment:</u> Having a very poor mentor or no mentor at all. Opportunities lost or never arisen; stress, overwork, a feeling of drifting and aimlessness. Having no hope that one's profession or craft will ever yield satisfaction or success.

XVIII: The Moon

Upright: Fearful Passage

General: Fear, anxiety, dread, dreams, nightmares, hallucinations, confusion. Trepidation or long-building anxiety over having to face something difficult. Threatening or woeful premonitions. Surrealness and strangeness. Regrets, nostalgias. Being frozen or unable to act on something. Phantoms, ghosts, hauntings. Facing situations or fears that, while difficult, lead to liberation. Resolving spiritual debts to the deep. Sacrifice. Learning from strange teachers.

State of Mind or Soul: The difficulty of having to face the hard truth about something. Confronting fearful situations or dealing with fear. Interior paralysis. Feeling existential dread. Intuitions that can be disturbing but contain crucial insights. Trance states or visionary states.

Relational: Having to face hard truths about a partner or allies. Being in denial about something important in a relationship or partnership. Fearing a partner or people one is bonded to. Strange situations that put people in strange places. Unreliable behaviors between people or murky communication. Feeling lost within relationships. Living in the past.

Employment: Fear of lacking in performance or personal productivity, fear of losing one's job or not succeeding at needful challenges. Anxiety in workplace or workspaces, or in meeting deadlines or quotas. Feeling confused or unclear about what is expected or needed. Feeling unfocused or lacking in energy for efforts.

Reversed: Fearful Imprisonment

General: Mental illness, harmful and chronic anxieties, living trapped in fear, or having to endure desperately unclear or confusing situations. Threatening situations and unpredictability. Being made to face fears or challenges that one cannot handle at present. Depression about the past. Loss of the ability to comprehend reality. Choosing to live in fantasies that protect one from fear or truth. Inability to give up something important. Hiding from fears.

State of Mind or Soul: Being overwhelmed by fears or confusions. Loss of control. Internal slavery to feelings of dread or darker forces without names. Spiritual dread. Interior torment or disquiet of various kinds. Emotional instability.

Relational: Inability to communicate with partners or allies. Fear of intimate partners or allies that turns into resentment or rivalry. Confusion between persons. Too many secrets kept and too many deceits that turn into a nigh-unrecoverable situation.

Employment: Having to deal with the negative consequences of one's previous performance or actions, or the negative consequences of other people's dealings and doings. Hostile workplaces, chaotic situations, inability to perform due to stress or anxiety. A bad situation that seems to create fear or resentment. Lack of returns.

XIX: The Sun

Upright: Sublime Joy and Peace

General: Liberation, joy, peace, happiness, resolution of pain or problems, joy of relating, belonging, great relief or serenity. Success. Realization of the most critical or fundamental things. Healing.

State of Mind or Soul: Being wise, feeling connected, and being at peace with the world. Feeling resolved to a formerly difficult situation, with great happiness at the resolution. True "individuation" in the relational, primordial sense of a functioning, whole mind or being in conscious relationship to all else. Love of life. Serenity.

Relational: Great enjoyment of partners or allies. Love, happiness and warm, beneficial exchanges. Relationships free from bickering, power-games, unwise declarations, blames, or guilt. Problems resolved.

Employment: Success at work or on projects, knowing that one is fulfilling their vocation or task in life, honors, promotions, praise, great satisfaction in efforts.

Reversed: Contentment

<u>General:</u> Same as the previously given upright meanings, with the addition that a person must trust in the Fitness of Things to shine through and lead to resolution for difficult situations.

<u>State of Mind or Soul:</u> Being very close to realizing the truth of inter-relatedness and interbeing, close enough to intellectualize it and gain a degree of peace from it, but not yet enough to feel it entirely. Being close to truth, and living in the warmth of truth as it unfolds. Being on the right path. Feeling optimistic and hopeful. Feeling peaceful and even sentimental. Enjoying life.

<u>Relational:</u> Same as the previously given upright meanings, with the addition that situations between allies or partners contain within themselves the seeds of great breakthroughs and happiness, even when difficult times are upon them.

<u>Employment:</u> Same as the previously given upright meanings, with the addition that one should be aware that the natural up's and down's of joy and difficulty in any profession or art (so long as they aren't born in maliciousness or the sickness of a broken system) are natural and normal and fit into a larger rightness.

XX: Judgement

Upright: Regeneration or Rebirth

<u>General:</u> Rebirth, regeneration, transformation, initiation, new beginnings, renewed faith or hope, renewal, spiritual attainment or development, finding new freedoms from new perspectives. New alliances possible.

<u>State of Mind or Soul:</u> Feeling like a new person. Being unattached to one outcome or another, and thus at peace with anything that happens. Feeling naturally, easily happy and content. Seeing a bigger picture. Feeling like one understands something or many things, and possessing confidence thereby. Feeling inspired. Feeling eager to live and interact with the world and others.

<u>Relational:</u> The springtime of a new relationship or partnership. Trying new things with partners, overcoming problems and feeling like a relationship has been renewed thereby. A new love or lover, a new ally, a new person coming into one's life, relationship, or family.

<u>Employment:</u> Gaining new organization, using or learning new tactics or skills, gaining advanced training that puts a person in a new echelon of skill. A great change in one's approach to work, or even a change in profession/job, but one that leads to new and better places. Worldly changes that make a field or task more viable or exciting or profitable.

Reversed: Decay or Stasis

<u>General:</u> Stasis, decay, failure to change when needed or necessary, failure to grow or thrive. Failure to become enflamed or enthusiastic. A situation that lingers and won't end or change. Hardship in maintaining faith or hope in things. Spiritual tedium or a withering away of motivation, whether spiritual or otherwise. Inability to see new perspectives. Being stuck.

<u>State of Mind or Soul:</u> Feeling dull or bored inside. Feeling as though one doesn't know where to go, or that one cannot grow or change. EnnuI: Feelings of disquiet. Inability to see any "bigger pictures." Feeling uninspired or unable to become inspired.

<u>Relational:</u> The autumn of a relationship, the fading feelings between people, allies, or partners. Relationships that are stuck in one place, unable to advance or change in needful ways. Someone leaving a relationship or partnership or alliance; people vanishing or leaving or drifting away.

<u>Employment:</u> Being victimized by useless or inefficient organizational realities, refusal or inability to learn new skills or tactics. Failing to gain training or skill that is necessary for advancement or accomplishment. Blockage for efforts. Systemic problems that cause a field to become difficult or viable. Potential loss of job or hindrance to career path.

XXI: The World

Upright: Great Good

General: Blissful joy, happiness, best of luck, completion, completeness, contentment and fulfillment, rapture, knowing the truth, being free and unburdened. Health and well-being. Natural beauty. Success.

State of Mind or Soul: The state of a realized person- being filled with peace and consciously enjoying harmony between oneself and all else. No longer being obsessed by or tormented by confusions within oneself, and feeling open and fearless. Being able to see the whole, to see the fitness or deeper meanings of things that occur, for good or for ill. Wisdom. True happiness. The ability to mentally and emotionally overcome any challenge or pain.

Relational: Unconditional love, benevolence, or patience between partners or allies. Truly healthy interactions that benefit all. Fulfillment between people. Finding the way together. Overcoming any challenges and becoming closer for it.

Employment: Loving one's work, and excelling at it. Accomplishing one's task in life through work or creativity. Being a great boon to the people around you, who interact with you in this capacity. Making things better for oneself and others. Life satisfaction.

Reversed: Great Good

<u>General:</u> Same as the previously given upright meanings, with the addition that a person must trust in the Fitness of Things to shine through and lead to resolution during difficult situations.

<u>State of Mind or Soul:</u> Same as the previously given upright meanings.

<u>Relational:</u> Same as the previously given upright meanings.

<u>Employment:</u> Same as the previously given upright meanings.

III.

The Counsel of the Cards

The Fool

Upright: Counsels a new beginning, trying something new in this situation. Warns against absent-mindedness or not taking something seriously enough with regards to your situation.

Reversed: Counsels seeking allies or outside guidance because the situation may be beyond your ability to handle alone. Warns against overconfidence and not paying attention to very small details.

The Sorcerer

Upright: Counsels bringing creativity and skill to bear on a situation in a very firm and motivated way. Warns against excessive manipulation or insincerity with other people or beings.

Reversed: Counsels thinking outside the box and not trying things you've tried already in a situation. Warns about lies or manipulations that you may be the victim of unawares, or of things unknown to you that you need to discover.

The Sorceress

Upright: Counsels seeking extraordinary guidance through esoteric means. Warns against trying to over-rationalize or over-think a situation.

Reversed: Counsels to accept that things may not go your way, and considering alternative goals that can still yield peace for you. Warns against obsessing over an issue and looking at the bigger picture as much as you can.

The Empress

Upright: Counsels relaxing, lightening up, embracing pleasures, and trusting in growth. Warns against missing the great things the present has to offer or being stingy.

Reversed: Counsels taking time to heal and get stronger. Warns against distractions, total surrender, or inaction.

The Emperor

Upright: Counsels clarifying what you need or want and becoming assertive. Warns against being so aggressive or driven that people become alienated or resentful.

Reversed: Counsels joining forces with others and empowering them to help you. Warns against trying to over-control situations and against egomania.

The Pope

Upright: Counsels getting good advice from others and doing things the reliable, old fashioned way. Warns against rocking the boat too much or being too eccentric in one's approach.

Reversed: Counsels examining things to ensure clarity and worthiness for your goals and convictions, and being sincere. Warns against being too rigid in how one approaches things, and against being arrogant.

The Lovers

Upright: Counsels making allies and being passionate about what you do in this situation- putting real love and passion into it. Warns against believing that this situation can be resolved too early, or can be resolved quickly.

Reversed: Counsels that you compromise and not let emotions run too high, if possible. Warns against acting from a place of jealousy or insecurity.

The Chariot

Upright: Counsels not waiting and making progress on your issue right now, any way you can. Warns against making excuses not to move or act.

Reversed: Counsels looking for alternative ways forward. Warns against trusting only your own judgment to find a good way ahead or imagining that just because you have an enormous motivation or energy, that you will get everything you want.

Justice

Upright: Counsels looking at your situation from another perspective, a more objective one, and not hiding from the truths about it. It also insists that a person demand what is truly owed to them, and let themselves be angry at injustices truly done to them, if it is relevant. Warns against thinking that one can win if one is not worthy to win, deep down.

Reversed: Counsels resolving yourself fairly to any persons or powers that you have emotional, spiritual, or tangible personal debts with. Warns against thinking that you can escape from the imbalances that may exist within your situation by ignoring them.

The Hermit

Upright: Counsels taking time to get some space and some peace and think things through, very deeply, before doing anything else. Warns against acting too quickly, and against being too bitter and letting resentment shape one's perspective.

Reversed: Counsels not giving up and seeing this situation as an opportunity to test one's skill and explore one's limits. Warns against letting insecurity or fear dominate one's thinking or acting.

The Wheel of the World

Upright: Counsels being thankful for what advantages one already has, and being ready to participate in the larger changes around oneself that are occurring now and which are coming. Warns against wanting or yearning beyond one's realistic ability or expectations.

Reversed: Counsels not letting bad luck break one's spirit, and seeking alternative ways of securing one's plans. Warns against being impatient and trying to handle more than one human being can handle.

Strength

Upright: Counsels finding aid from a good, skilled, or powerful outside source to help in making your next decisive step. Warns against thinking that brute strength, personal skill, or ordinary thinking can overcome the challenge you're facing.

Reversed: Counsels discovering and reducing one's vulnerabilities and trying to avoid situations of being alone or working alone. Warns against rugged individualism or trying to force one's personal way of thinking onto others or the situation.

The Hanged Man

Upright: Counsels being very flexible with one's approach, and counsels knowing how to deal with pain and suffering, which often means accepting painful things outside of your conscious control. Warns against excessive compromise or giving too much of oneself away to anything.

Reversed: Counsels looking towards very real alternatives, including changes of plans as far as they can be made. Warns against insisting that this situation go forward as expected and thinking that one is stronger than they really are.

Death

Upright: Counsels that something very important must be released or let go before progress will be possible. Warns against being in denial about what has to change and warns against avoiding uncomfortable things.

Reversed: Counsels that one prepare for not having all the allies or resources one believed would be present in this situation. Warns against believing that your situation will be resolved by easy efforts or getting one's hopes too far up.

Temperance

Upright: Counsels that one trust in helpers or allies, and assume a balanced approach in all efforts at present- make concessions to keep things even or balanced on all sides. Warns against being greedy or egotistical.

Reversed: Counsels being receptive, making friends or helpers happy, and making efforts to keep them that way. Warns against allowing stress or anxiety to override your thinking or destroy your peace.

The Devil

Upright: Counsels that you think outside of the box, prepare for wild, unpredictable things, and not see the wild or unpredictable things as your enemies. Warns against doubting or trying to repress one's own natural desires or impulse towards freedom and satisfaction.

Reversed: Counsels working to understand what binds you and others in this situation, and dealing with those things fairly and wisely before trying to force any issues. Warns against underestimating how destructive or surprising the hidden things in your situation can be, and how they always have a way of emerging, no matter how well you plan.

The Ruined Tower

Upright: Counsels having an open mind, making at least one big change in one's perspective or situation if at all possible (even if it's uncomfortable), and being as flexible as possible otherwise. Warns against identifying to much with, or relying too much upon, things the way they are.

Reversed: Counsels that a person become prepared now for big changes or difficulties. Warns against underestimating just how devastating or demoralizing sudden changes can be, and how disappointing things can be as they work out in ways beyond our control.

The Star

Upright: Counsels being optimistic and hopeful, and remembering how many friends, allies, and blessings one has had in the past, and has now. Warns against thinking that just hope is enough to get through a situation; one must also do wise things and be generous to others.

Reversed: Counsels doing everything one can do to avoid falling into despair; find joyful relations and activities and take shelter in their warmth. Warns against acting like you don't care or that things don't matter. Look closely- many things matter.

The Moon

Upright: Counsels facing something you fear and committing yourself to dealing with it. Warns against any story or idea that tries to make legitimately fearful things seem less fearful.

Reversed: Counsels that you face a hard truth as soon as you can, without delay. Warns against getting swept up in hardships or obsessing over traumas, fears, and pains to the point that you can't move forward or face things with an open mind and courage.

The Sun

Upright: Counsels that you follow and trust what makes you joyful or happy, especially in conjunction with others, and let those feelings make you strong. Warns against letting oneself fall into bad situations or negative thinking because of old habits or laziness.

Reversed: Counsels the same as "upright", but also that you look to how much good exists inside yourself and this world, and be unafraid to be happy. Warns against being pessimistic or shut off from your surroundings.

Judgement

Upright: Counsels embracing a new change or a new direction. Warns against mindlessly staying the same as before or hoping for things to return to how they once were.

Reversed: Counsels that one strive to realize that hope and happiness come in cycles, and aren't always present, and to be patient with oneself and others. Warns against throwing out good future opportunities because of disillusionment or discomfort with the present.

The World

Upright: Counsels that one stay where they are, doing what they're doing, with great hope, or to follow one's feelings or any obvious good signs that are telling one what to do. Warns against being too shut away or isolated.

Reversed: Counsels same as above, but further insists that one trust themselves and the world. Warns against thinking that one great moment or happy period is the whole of life's joy.

IV.

Methodology:

The Oracle and the Vision of Cartomancy

When one seeks to have a genuine experience of divination, it is necessary to create a situation in which other-than-human or other-than-conscious persons and forces can get a message, a vision, or a sign from their extraordinary way of being into our ordinary one. Some forms of divination find ways around this "gap" in receiving things and simply plunge the diviner or the person seeking the divination into the extraordinary world, to receive directly. A good example of that would be dream divination in which divinatory dreams are incubated, allowing a person in the deep trance of sleep to receive of the strange powers more directly.

Cartomancy- divination with cards- is a method of "bridging the gap" between this world and the other, or (alternatively) between what a human experiences as their surface consciousness and deeper reaches inside themselves. The otherworld is more than just the depths of the human mind, though the depths of the mind act as a connective point between us and It.

For modern people who may be uncomfortable with the idea of an objectively-existing Otherworld, or simply incapable of grasping the entire concept in a natural, anxiety-free way, it helps to do as some popular schools of depth psychology have done and simply consider the Unseen World to be the depths of a personal or collective unconscious. I personally view this as an intermediate stage in coming to eventually comprehend the deep for what it really is: something that does objectively exist, and is far older than humankind as we know it now.

In a way, all real divination is an act of oracle-seeking and oracle-obtaining. An oracle is a person, a place, or a thing (and sometimes a combination of them) that allows for an other-than-human person or power to give messages to human beings. It is a person, a place, or a thing that can create a situation through which a communication from the extraordinary world can be mediated to the ordinary.

History tells of certain very powerful oracles, which had national and cultural importance to many people, such as the famed Oracle at Delphi. At Delphi, a woman, made sacred through the inhalation of special gasses rising from a rift in the earth in a very sacred place was granted visions that she then communicated in a highly esoteric form to people who came from all over the world.

She answered their questions in this manner, but it was not she that was the source of the answers. In later times, it was the God Apollo, though the sacred site of the Oracle was not originally devoted to Apollo. It was originally devoted to the great Earth Mother, the Earth Indweller, and guarded by a powerful serpent. Whoever was giving the visions to the Pythia (the oracle-priestess) the fame of the place was great.

Oracles allowing powerful spirits or Gods to give messages to human beings were fairly common in the ancient world. Not all were quite as "large" or involved as the Delphi oracle. Some were personal activities, like the cast of dice or lots, that allowed for a person or small groups of people to obtain guidance from an entity or non-human person that they had some kind of relationship with. The idea of using an oracular device to speak with the depths of oneself, in some depth-psychology sort of way, is a modern idea. In ancient times, devices of divination and oracles aimed at other entities apart from a man or woman, such as their deceased family members, the gods or protective spirits of one's family or village or community.

Some modern people may choose to think (pursuant to our habit of re-writing or accommodating history to suit what we want to believe) that our Ancestors were always receiving messages from themselves without realizing it. Some modern people may believe that our Ancestors simply couldn't see through their cultural beliefs about spirits and Gods enough to see this truth or that the Gods and Spirits were nothing more than aspects of their minds. I sternly reject these re-appraisals of history and speak from many years of experience when I cite my belief that otherworldly entities are real and complete persons, and not merely faces of the human personal unconscious.

I don't bring this controversial topic up to inspire acrimony; I bring it up because I believe a very real degree of respect and reverence is required to approach an oracle. I further believe that the kind of respect we pay to beings we identify as other persons is different from the respect we pay to encounters we label as aspects of ourselves. From the practical perspective of gaining authentic and truthful divinatory messages, we do better when we let ourselves really encounter the sources of those messages as completely individual beings that do not rely upon us as the source of their primary existence.

In a sense, every being relies on others for its existence; this is one of the crucial insights of Interbeing. However, in the act of divination-seeking, it's best to approach the situation as though one is approaching a venerable elder being who was around long before oneself, and whose knowledge, personality and character greatly stands in a mysterious manner beyond oneself. Instead of seeing them as an aspect of the personal or unconscious self, it's better to understand them as part of the same great system of Interbeing to which you both belong. Being extraordinary beings, they indwell that system in such a manner as to have greater or deeper insights and (we hope) the potential for benevolence, and a willingness to relate to you.

The key to authentic divination comes down to just these things: the amount of genuine respect and reverence you put into it and the amount of time and effort you put into it. This element of time and effort cannot be understated. All things held equal, simply putting ten minutes aside to shuffle some cards and lay out a spread will never be able to yield the kinds of results that devoting three hours to the effort will.

Devoting three hours to being alone with oneself and the oracle gives much time for insight. Spending the first hour simply relaxing and focusing on the many angles of one's question, or examining the confusion or difficulties one is facing, then spending an hour studying the cards in sequence, and finally devoting the last hour to making reverential requests (with one's voice or in one's heart) to the sources of the divination really sets a powerful stage.

If this is done before randomizing the cards and selecting the ones chosen by the source to spell out your answer, it has high potential for connection and accuracy. It is potent in a way far beyond anything ten minutes or thirty minutes could yield.

And the more time put aside, the more powerful it becomes. Removing oneself to the company of the oracle for an entire day of contemplation, study, devotion, and divination could yield incredible and life-altering results. One always gets out of this experience what one is willing to put in.

If a deep relationship with a source or sources of divination is created and maintained, then the ability to do emergency divinations in a brief amount of time becomes a possibility. But before such relationships are formed, divination must be a thoughtful thing that diviners put a good quantity of extraordinary effort and attention into.

The source of divinatory insight is a topic that must be considered now, and considered carefully. In ordinary sorcerous terms (sorcery being the art of bonding or allying oneself with familiar spirits, for various ordinary and extraordinary purposes) most divinations are done with the aid of a spirit called a divining familiar.

A sorcerer or sorceress spends a goodly amount of time gaining the boon of such an entity, finding and allying with them for the purpose of empowering divinations in the future, and paying for that boon in various ways. This present work is not the place to cover the entire extraordinary sequence of methods and possible means for gaining such a familiar spirit, but it is enough to mention that the divining familiar is a common source for divinations among witches or sorcerously-active persons.

Many of the people reading this book and preparing to approach this oracle may not be sorcerously active in this way and may not yet have the power to obtain a divining familiar, if ever. This is not any sort of problem because sources of divination are many. And there is a particular source- a powerful other-than-human person- that we encountered when reading through the Narrative chapter of this book which I believe everyone should attempt to reach when using this oracle or any oracle like it.

And that person is the Follower-Entity that accompanies each person through their life in this world. In Mystery XI, Strength, that being appeared in the form of an animal. In Mystery XIV, Temperance, it appeared as a human being. This Follower, or Fetch as it is also called, is ordinarily only met during times of high danger or stress during the human life and then at death, where it acts as a guide or psychopomp for the journeying person into the beyond. To gain full conscious knowledge of the animal and human forms of this entity before death- and to begin to interact regularly with it- is a reversal of the natural order of things, a powerful otherworldly event that makes a man or woman into a sorcerer.

But an oracle seeker need not go that far to cultivate a relationship that can allow for extraordinary personal insights gained from divination. Even without a face-to-face meeting with the Follower, even without knowledge of their many forms or a fully conscious awareness of it, the Follower is still always there. It is usually unable to be seen or consciously felt, but it does actively aid a person in life through the gifts of dreams at important times and feelings or intuitions of danger, given as warnings at other times. If a person is seriously ill or injured, it may intervene to save a person or help them recover. It works tirelessly to protect its human partner until the fateful time of death is at hand, at which point it activates to help in a new and very important way.

The Follower is always there, no matter how unconscious ordinary people may be of it. It is there and aware in its own way of what we are feeling and doing. When we have strong needs, we can open ourselves to the possibility of its presence and ask it directly to help guide divinations for us, giving it an opportunity to spell out messages for us. We can trust that it has our best interests in mind, and (insofar as we are able to receive its messages) will not lead us astray.

To cultivate a relationship with the Follower begins with recognizing it and believing that it is there. The annals of folklore and myth make it clear that this belief is not in vain. One need not visualize it in any given way, unless one desires to. If one orients their mind and heart towards it and reaches out with deep desire from inside, it will know, it will see, and it will begin the process of responding on the many levels it might. The words one might use as a request for divination from the Follower are very simple and to the point:

> "Follower of my soul, protector of my soul and my life-house, you who accompany me through the seasons of this life, hear me. See me. Preserve me. Guide me. In dreams, appear as you can or will. In waking, let my skin feel the pressure of your touch. In my times of need, guide my hands and mind to select the cards of this oracle that I most need to see, to comprehend your guidance for me."

Within this short invocation are also words that might be re-worked as a general prayer for connection, which might be chanted daily, many times a day, to cultivate inside one's mind and awareness a sense for the subtle presence of the Follower. One can offer gifts to the Follower, too- bowls of cream, fruits, honey, blood drawn from one's own left hand. What you're willing to put into it has everything to do with what you will get out, over time.

While cultivating a relationship with the personal soul-follower might well take on dimensions that modern people would identify as "religious", there are other sources of divination that will easily fall into the category of religious devotion or spirituality, as it is ordinarily understood. Persons sincerely devoted to nearly any religion, and who have sufficiently open minds, might trust in the entities they are religiously devoted to with regards to gaining guidance through divination.

Mainstream religions like Christianity or Islam strictly forbid such acts, so devoted Christians or Muslims who seek to utilize divination are either sideways (in some fashion) from the mainstream of their own faiths, or perhaps they've become desperate. It's true that, unofficially, divination has been practiced by members of mainstream faiths throughout the history of those faiths. How a person justifies it to themselves really is up to them.

With sufficient belief that their God, or whomever may guide them via a divination device like Tarot, those persons might gain a potential source of divination, though who can say? If God turns his face away from people seeking occult means to address problems, perhaps the Follower or someone else could step into the open space of need and answer the call.

Those who belong to non-mainstream religions or spiritual paths that have room for divination will discover that the Gods or spirits or entities otherwise to whom they are devoted are almost certain to respond to sincerely offered reverence and sincerely expressed need. Again, if they do not do it themselves, perhaps other sympathetic powers in their service, or powers connected to the diviner, might step in to complete the connection and grant messages.

In the heart of the old Fayerie Faith, which is a name given to the localized, organic, and animistic-type relationship system that people around the British Isles and Europe once experienced in conjunction with the spirits and powers of their landscapes (and which transmitted itself to the Americas and to other places) there exists a potential for devotional relationship with the King and Queen of Spirits- the King and Queen of the Fayerie-World, which is the Underworld or the world of the dead, at least from our living perspective. The

Fayerie Faith isn't primarily about such Lordly figures as these two, but it must include them in its own folkloric cosmology.

The Fayerie Faith is just as devoted to (if not more devoted to) nameless local spirits, and others who definitely have names and folklorically recorded personalities and features. But all of these powers are expressions of otherworldly overlap, through the land, with this world, and otherworldly relationships being formed by people in this world with "Them Over There."

If a person cultivates relationships with the spirits of the land upon which one lives, those spirits can be respectfully approached and asked to communicate to a person in terms of divination. Not all spirits have the extraordinary kind of insight or wisdom to answer the hard questions that a human being might have, but all spirits still exist in a condition that defies our ordinary expectations, and many seem to have foresight of various kinds or degrees. Others may be very wise indeed, especially those connected to powerful places like mountains or rivers or old forests.

The realities of how such relationships are cultivated transcend the scope of this work, but they do not transcend the scope of what a person's intuition probably tells them already. Being present in places like that, regularly giving offerings, being respectful, acknowledging the presence of such powers, being generous with those offerings, and protecting the plants and animals that dwell in such a place is how a person really enters into real relationship with them.

To aim devotion towards their King and Queen- the two most potent Indwellers that we met in the Tarot Narrative (They are none other than the Master entity that often appeared as a serpent in our Major Arcana cards, and the Earth Indweller herself who appeared in many cards such as The Empress and The Star) is a way of actualizing the Fayerie Faith's primordial essence within oneself and perhaps gaining the favor of these great powers, such that they or their duly-appointed emissaries will act as a divination source for you.

There is a ritual that one might perform to potentially gain the attentions of these mighty otherworldly beings. If it is done before a Tarot divination, and if They reach out, the messages spelled out will be meaningful and truthful. Before I outline the simple form of the ritual (and one must feel free to intuitively deepen it or alter it as one sees fit) I must reiterate that what you put into these things has an important relationship to what you get out. Respect and reverence for these entities must come first. He is the secret Master of life; She is ultimately the grandmother of souls and the source of the food and water that human beings need to live, and the source of all the entities that we share our world with. If They are not due the highest reverence, then no being is.

Taking oneself aside to a private place and time, removing distractions, and devoting as much time as possible to this effort, one should place two long sticks peeled of their bark (preferably) in the shape of an equal-armed cross on a table or a bare floor or bare ground. In the four square spaces created by the equal-armed cross (between its legs) a white or black stone should be placed. If working by night, only natural light (as from fires or candles) should ever be used. One should gaze steadily upon the formation made of sticks and stones, relax oneself, and let oneself feel only the sensation of the body. The operant should simply abide in that sensation, whatever it may be. The sensation will begin to relax and shift. Use a lancet or a very sharp and clean knife to coax some droplets of blood from your left hand and smear the blood-offering of yourself onto the four stones.

These words might be used to proceed:

> "Oberyon, great king of spirits, old serpent, ancient white one, I offer blood to you as a reverent sacrifice, and beg for your graces from Below. I say these powerful words to gain your attentions: Bentranas, Bethaca, Benedill, Pantangor, Petangor, Damadas, Penedill, Paentagoras, Amadas, Oberyon, Rex Lewsydission. From your royal throne, look upon me always. Be kind and grant me your aid in the divination I am about to perform forthwith. If it pleases you, send one of your serving men to guide my hands and mind to discover the truth from these cards of divination."

Then, relax a bit longer and say

> "Titam, great queen of the little folk below, beautiful, terrible, and awe-inspiring Lady of Elfhame, I offer this blood to you as a reverent sacrifice, and beg for your graces from below. I say the names of your serving ladies, your seven devoted maidens who surround you and follow the direction of your will always, in the hopes that you will permit them to attend my divination here and guide it well. Lillia is the first named, Restillia the second, Foca the third, Folla the fourth, Afryca the fifth, Julia the sixth, and Venulla the seventh."

At this point, put another dab of your blood in the bottom of a bowl and fill that bowl with fresh full cream or deep red port wine and hold it over the cross of wood you made, declaring it an offering to the powers that indwell the land, and to their great King and Queen. Ask them to wish you no ill and do you no harm. Then put the bowl down on the other side of the cross from you. As soon as your work here is done, that bowl should be poured out onto bare earth somewhere or at the roots of a tree. The sticks and stones, if possible, should be returned respectfully to a forest or the land.

(Note: in the invocations above, one must aspire to pronounce these names as well and smoothly as one can. The word "Lewsydission" is pronounced "Leh-oo-suh-DEE-see-on." The Fayerie Maiden Afryca's name is pronounced "uh-FRICK-uh." Titam's name is pronounced "TIE-tam") Pronounce the rest as best you may, and so long as you are genuinely reverential, all will be well.)

Using the ritual outline given above, one can do more than just seek a source for divination, or a boon from these powers. One can build a relationship with them, over time and with sincere devotion. That may be the most important or valuable thing a wise man or woman ever does, for the Good Indwelling Powers respond favorably to sincere and lengthy devotion and can pour out many blessings of luck into a person's life and death.

Another important source for divination can be one's deceased relatives or friends. Having gone beyond themselves, the portion of them that survives the passage of death can become wise and insightful in ways beyond our living comprehension. You can cultivate relationships with them easily, so long as you had fairly close bonds in life. Regularly visiting their graves, burial sites, or remains is crucial, as is giving them offerings of honey, cream, or wine. To attempt to approach them as sources of divination always works best at night, and always best if you are as close to their burial sites or remains as you can be.

Respectfully taking a small portion of their grave-earth, if they have graves, and keeping it in a jar which is opened during divinations can help. Also, the anniversary day and night of their deaths is the best time for reaching out to them, and the closer in the year that time is, the better. There are certain traditional times of year (the Twelve Nights of Yule, and the entire first week of November) in which the dead were thought more able to interact with the living, so those make ideal times to respectfully approach them as well.

In the night, only by candle-light, and having cultivated the above, one can call upon them by saying their full names aloud and begging for their aid and support. One must cultivate a sense of openness to their subtle presence and proceed with the divination as usual afterwards.

The sources of divination that I have described above are the ones I suggest the most. For those who cannot or will not utilize them in some form or fashion, the final option is to rely entirely upon the depths of oneself and be radically open to those depths. Focus, in a quiet place, upon your own depths while randomizing and selecting the cards. Focusing on getting a message from the portion of you below your rational mind that may know hidden things regarding situations you need help or guidance with.

The most important thing in this method- as it is in any of the methods described above- is to take time to really think about your situation, and visualize all of the aspects of it- the people involved, the outcomes that one fears or desires, the confusions one feels, or anything else.

When you have done this, and always in a place where you can be alone and have some measure of peace, you must form the question you really wish to ask. You can never ask for an answer to a question that you already know the answer to. This will invalidate the reading. You can never ask the same question twice, until a sufficient and significant amount of time has passed since you asked, and things in the situation have changed somewhat. Also, you must never ask for an answer to a question that you truly don't want to hear an answer for. Trust your instincts here- not all questions need to be answered.

With the Tarot oracle, I strongly suggest that you seek answers in one of two forms. Seek to discover what hidden forces are playing upon a presently-existing situation, whether inside yourself or others or just the situation as a whole. Or, seek to know how in some near or distant future forces will be existing around a situation that is playing out at present.

For example, if you wish to know what it is inside yourself that is causing you to hesitate or feel afraid in some situation, that can be revealed. The same can be revealed about other people. If you wish to know the state of mind of another person or their physical, tangible condition in many other ways, that can be asked.

Using the oracle to study one's condition of soul deep down is important; but one can never ask the oracle how one is consciously feeling at present because you *already know* how you are consciously feeling at present. Discovering how the deeper levels of the self are acting and being acted upon, however, can help shed light on things you do feel at times, or other situations occurring in one's life.

If you are facing a difficult challenge in the coming days or months and wish to know how that is going to play out, that can be revealed. If you are worried over the outcome of a situation that is not played out yet, how it is most likely to play out can be revealed.

And lastly, if you wish counsel on how to deal with a hard situation you are in, that can be given with relative ease. I will now describe some methods of laying the cards out and gaining their messages.

Method I. The Single Card Reading

No matter what method you are utilizing, **always randomize and select your cards in this fashion**: hold all 22 in your hand, face down. None of the cards in your hand should be reversed. Shuffle them once. Deal out five, face down, before you.

These five are the "starters" of five piles. Deal out the next five onto the backs of those starters, still face down. Don't put them down in the same order that you placed the starters; without thinking about it, put the next five each randomly upon a starter.

Then, turn the next five cards in your hand upside down. Put these five upside down cards randomly upon the five stacks on the table in front of you (by doing this, you are inserting some reversed cards.) Then, put the next five in your hand (these won't be reversed) upon the five stacks, and then you should have two cards left in your hand.

Put those two on any of the stacks you want. Pick up all the stacks and shuffle again. Now, fan out the cards as neatly as you can. You are prepared to select from the fan the cards you need. Always randomize like this each time you ask a new question or seek a counsel.

In the case of the one card spread, you'll only be selecting one, so put out your left hand, empty your mind of thoughts, and simply select any card. Don't think about it too long; don't think about it at all, if you can help it. Just gaze briefly upon the fan and take a card. Trust the source of your divination to lead your hand right where it needs to go- "I cannot select the wrong card" must be your firm belief.

Look at the card you selected. Depending on what you asked, it is revealing to you some hidden fact about your own depths, or the conscious state or depths of another person, if that interested you (or them.) It may be showing you *what will be* when a certain situation plays itself out, or how a certain situation will be a week from now, a month from now, or even just tomorrow.

If you wanted a one-card sign for how a job interview tomorrow was going to go, and you got The Empress reversed, you would look at the general meaning, and then at the "employment" column, and you'd see that things aren't looking great for that interview. It might be worth your time to do a second reading for advice on how to possibly mitigate that bad situation.

If you got the Empress upright, it looks like the signs for the interview are quite favorable. If the meanings you find for your cards are overall positive, it's just looking good. If they are neutral or negative, well, anything might happen.

Whether your card is right-side up or reversed, you can look at the meanings chapter to get quite a list of different possible meanings. Select one thing or a few things from the meanings given there, as your intuition guides you, or your source guides you.

If you described a situation and wanted advice, turn to the chapter entitled "The Counsel of the Cards" and find your result there. A word of caution needs to be sounded here and for all attempts to look up card meanings on lists of meanings. While the "Counsel of the Cards" chapter may, at times, give you just the advice you need in a situation, sometimes the advice from a card can be gained just from gazing at the card itself. Remember, you must be flexible.

When you look at the card, (turn it right-side up if it was reversed) what things on the card do you find your eyes being drawn to over and over again? What did you really look at first? What does the image feel like it is saying? You can get counsel in these ways, without even needing to look at the Counsel entries given in this book. You can get shades of meaning or messages in this way that might be more relevant to you than what's listed in the Meaning entries.

The only thing you must never do is change your mind and seek counsel in another way, once you've committed to using a particular method. If you committed yourself to looking up Counsel from the book, then what the book told you is your answer. You can't decide to try to get intuitive counsel after reading the counsel you got, which is usually done in hopes of getting an answer you'd prefer.

Another means of gaining Counsel- and this may be the single best method- is to read the Narrative associated with the card that you got as a Counsel and look at what topics the Narrative discusses. It may be trying to tell you to focus on one or more of those topics or ideas, or urging you to craft your solution from the inspiration you get from reading the

Narrative section of the card. Again, in this method of counsel seeking, it matters not if the drawn card was reversed.

Sometimes people desire to ask "yes or no" questions- like "Should I take this stranger up on his invitation to go out with him?" You discover whether or not the source of your divination thinks that's a good idea for you by looking at the meanings of the card that you pull. You phrase "yes/no" questions by framing them this way: "If I take up this man on his invitation to a social engagement tomorrow, what will come of that?"

Then, if the outcome looks bad, this is essentially the same as being told "No, you probably shouldn't go." If it looks good, that might be thought the same as a "yes, go." But one must never become so reliant upon sources of divination that they begin to ask about every single doubt they may have. That would quickly become too onerous and stressful, even on the relationship between the diviner and their source of divination. Try, as much as you are able, to make divination a special thing, only used when a situation or a question really troubles or concerns you.

With these basic notes, discovering the basics of the "shape of things to come" isn't such a hard task. If you're looking to see how your own health will play out in the next five years, simply asking "what will I be thinking and feeling about my condition of health in (x) years?" When you get your result, look at the column of meaning dealing with "state of mind or soul." It should be immediately clear if you'll be content with your health situation or not, just on a brief reading. This can be a helpful warning or a very calming insight, but if you're doing this right, you'll always be somewhat anxious to read about such things. Make sure you really want to know.

Method II. The Basic Three Card Reading

When the three cards are chosen for this method, turn them all facing up and see if any are reversed. If you have reversed cards, turn them back to right-side up but slide them down a little bit so that they sit slightly lower than the cards that were not reversed, so you remember they were reversed cards.

If all three cards are reversed, then turn them all back right-side up, but you'll just have to remember that they were all reversed when you interpret them. If you are photo-documenting these spreads, you can tilt all the cards slightly to the left to show they were all reversed.

When most people utilize three card readings, they are looking to the three cards to represent the "past, present, and future." And if you truly desire to do this, you can- only understand that the past and present cards must represent hidden layers of the past and present that you didn't know about and don't know about- for one can never ask about things they already know. The future card will represent what the dominant forces will be in the future of whatever situation you are asking about.

For me, the three card reading is about allowing the card in the center to reveal the dominant family of forces that is acting on a present situation in a hidden manner, or the dominant family for forces that will be acting upon the future of a situation, and allowing the cards to the right and left of it to be "attendants"- cards that will together modify the center card's meaning and give it new dimensions.

This isn't remotely as complicated as it may sound. The center card in the three card reading is just as I described above. Its attendants take their meanings and blend them together before applying their blended meaning directly to the center card. I will illustrate by example.

If you ask where your relationship with (x) person will be in one month's time, or in the coming year, or suchlike, and you draw The Wheel of the World upright for the center card, with The Fool upright to the left of it, and the Devil upright on the right, what you are seeing (after you reference the meanings chapter) is this:

Center: (Wheel of the World upright) **Good development**, happy turns in a relationship, feeling like one can be together a long time with another.

Left: (Fool upright) **Carefree**, spontaneity, enjoyment with partner.

Right: (Devil upright) **Wildness**, intoxication, strong emotions, being bound together, obsessions.

Now it's obvious that at first blush, things are going to be fine overall in your relationship with (x) in the future that you named. But as with all situations, it is surrounded by other powers and situations that are going to exert an influence on it. In this case, The Fool and The Devil represent the families of persons and powers that will be present, surrounding things in the future. They will affect things.

The upright Fool's influences are carefree, spontaneous enjoyment. The upright Devil's influences, however, are a touch more ominous or at least complicated- he brings in a wild element of emotions run strong and people becoming very attached to one another, bound together in some potentially weighty or darker ways. When we blend these two cards together, we get an image of people being a bit too carefree or not very mindful of their feelings for one another, or not mindful of dark emotional turns between them.

To say it more simply, these two cards might blend into the phrase "Carefree with strong emotions." It seems to suggest that you or your partner might start having some strong emotions that won't match what the other person is feeling, but this will be ignored or treated as though it's not any kind of issue worth dealing with.

Now, taking that blended meaning, we apply it back to the center. "Good development, a stable time together, but in the heart of this time, one or the other or both (of these partners) will be carefree and careless with some strong emotional developments." As you can see, the "good times to come" have this dark seed growing in their center. It stands to undermine the relationship's good times or stability, further on in the future.

There's already advice that can be extrapolated from this reading. From the warning given here comes the advice to watch how emotions develop and not be careless with them or mindless of them in the future. However, if one sees a particularly grim three card reading prognosticating ill things in the future, or even in the present, a one-card Counsel reading can be done to get some hints on how to deal with the situation when it arrives, or as it stands.

This method takes a goodly bit of practice, but I never found it to be very burdensome. Meanings blend together usually effortlessly if you allow them to. It does require some thought-experimentation or a touch of creativity, but you must never allow yourself to doubt yourself. Trust the sources of your divination to help guide your mind to come to the conclusions that they knew you would if they put these three cards before you.

It can seem difficult to "blend together" very positive qualities or meanings with very negative ones, when the cards require you to do so. There is a cunning tactic for resolving this difficulty. Take the meaning of the attendant on the right, and connect it to the meaning of the attendant on the left with the words "in the midst of" or just the word "in."

Alternatively, you can take the meaning of the attendant on the left and connect it to the meaning of the attendant on the right with the phrase "dependent upon." Try these combinations, and you will likely gain an insight into what the blended meanings point towards. One of the combinations will seize your intuitive attention.

Example: trying to blend together one of the meanings of Justice reversed (on the right) with The World upright (on the left) yields "Imbalance in the midst of Completeness" or "Completeness dependent upon Imbalance." An imbalance in the midst of a situation that seems very complete points to a dark secret, or something crucial that has been missed. A completeness that is based upon imbalance points to a sham completeness, a seemingly good state that relies upon hidden injustices or lopsided taking to maintain it.

Attempting to blend together a reversed Sorceress (on the right) with The Lovers upright (on the left) could yield "Unpredictability in attraction" or "Attraction dependent upon unpredictability." It's very clear what these statements can yield in the way of further meaning.

Method III: The Advanced Three Card Reading

In this method, the cards are allowed to potentially interact with one another in different ways than in the basic method. The card images themselves are brought even more to bear on how the reading will be interpreted.

Once you have gained your three cards, look at the center card. Then you must ask yourself what the center card does to or with the two attendant cards. It can do one of six things, and you will know upon looking at the center card which of the six it is:

1. The center card **Receives** the attendants: this means that the center card interacts with the two attendants in precisely the same way as explained in "The Basic Three Card Reading."

2. The center card **Round Tables** the attendants: this means that the center card stands alone, and the two attendants circle and orbit around it, creating an atmosphere for it. That atmosphere does not affect the center's meaning. The atmospheric forces do reveal things that might support the center's meaning, exist because of it, threaten it, or trouble it.

3. The center card **Integrates** the attendants: this means that the center card literally draws the two attendants together and forces them into a marriage of meaning. The center card's meaning doesn't matter for this reading- only the combined meanings of the attendants matters.

4. The center card **Instrumentalizes** the attendants: this means that the center card depicts a person holding things in their hands. For instance, The Justice card shows a woman holding a sword in her left hand and some scales in her right. If she's the center card, she instrumentalizes the attendants- the attendant closest to her sword becomes her sword, and

the attendant closest to her scales becomes the scales. This tells you something important about the meanings of her attendants- one will be the painful factor, and one will be the balancing factor in the situation being read about. Any figure holding any instrument (whether they only have one instrument, or two) can instrumentalize cards around them. The Emperor, though he usually Receives, can Instrumentalize his attendants by virtue of the fact that he has a pile of weapons to one side of him and a shield to his other side.

5. The center card **Is Crucified Between** the attendants: this formation only appears when The Hanged Man is the center card. This reveals a situation of crisis or transformation between two forces, the two forces being the attendants. The Hanged Man's meaning is irrelevant in this reading; only the two forces he's crucified or hung between matter. If he appears reversed in the center, simply treat him as right-side up.

6. The center card **Grasps** the attendants: this formation only appears when The Strength card is the center card. She takes the attendant behind her (the one to the left in the reading) and either uses it, or is using it, or will attempt to use it, to befriend or ally herself with the force before her (the attendant to the right.) This can show what's going to happen, what might should happen, or what is happening in a situation, for good or for ill. The Strength card's meaning is irrelevant in this reading; only the attendants matter. If she appears reversed in the center, simply treat her as right-side up.

In general, here are the cards that **Receive** their attendants: Death, The Emperor, The Empress, The Hermit, Judgement, The Sorceress, Temperance, The Star, The Sun, and The Ruined Tower.

Here are the cards that **Round Table** their attendants: The Moon, The Wheel of the World, and The World.

Here are the cards that **Integrate** their attendants: The Chariot, The Lovers, The Pope, and The Devil. The Empress can also integrate her attendants, pursuant to your intuition at the time of the reading.

Here are the cards that **Instrumentalize** their attendants: The Fool, Justice, and The Sorcerer. Death, The Devil, The Emperor, and The Pope might also do so, pursuant to your intuition at the time of the reading.

Here are the cards that **Are Crucified By** their attendants: The Hanged Man.

Here are the cards that **Grasp** their attendants: Strength.

"Dowsing" with the Major Arcana Cards

If one faces a difficult choice between two or more courses of action, and if a point of desperation with regard to determining which choice to make has been reached, the cards might be used to "dowse" or point the way to the best possible course of action to be followed. In this method, which should be used only as a last resort (and only if one intends to obey the result of the cards) is centered around The World card.

The World card always indicates a person or persons being in the right place, doing the right thing. Thus, you may write upon two separate sheets of paper or parchment the two options you can't decide between and place them to the east and west sides of room in which you divine, or to the east and west of a working area besides. If you have three or four options that you can't decide between, arrange them around you as equidistant from one another as possible. Four options (for instance) would be well-aligned to the north, south, east, and west of the diviner.

Imagine that small roads are connecting the diviner to each of the options. In the case of two options, two roads to the left and right of the diviner might be visualized, each ending at the papers written with the two options to be decided between. Once you have contacted the source of your divination, and done all that needs to be done, randomize the cards and begin laying them out, one at a time, on each of the "roads", alternating between them, one card on one, then one card on another. Continue to do this until The World card appears on one of the roads. The choice corresponding with that road is the choice the source of your divination has selected as being best for you at this point.

One might also "dowse" to discover the truth about events. If you are wondering if X event occurred or did not occur, you can write onto two papers or parchments "X event did occur" or "X event did not occur" and place them to the left and right of your working space. Then deal the randomized cards one at a time to your left and your right until The World card appears pointing towards the truth.

Discovering Concerns with the Cards

There may be times when the cards forecast some kind of problem or concern for you or for someone else at a future date, but the exact nature of that problem may be unknown to you, or unrevealed by the reading. If help is needed in discovering what the nature of an unknown concern may be, a card can be drawn as per the usual method (ignoring reversals) and this list consulted to help give clues towards the nature of the concern.

The Fool: Concerns life direction, knowing what you want, finding one's way, unburdening one's mind or soul.

The Sorcerer: Concerns being able to manipulate the system of one's life in a satisfying way, increasing one's skill. Can refer to employment.

The Sorceress: Concerns feeling spiritually satisfied or seeking explanations for strange experiences. Can also concern wanderlust or the strange urge to change.

The Empress: Concerns health issues, children, or the intricacies of romantic involvement.

The Emperor: Concerns being able to overcome challenges which are stopping one from feeling strong or in control. Can mean financial issues or legal ones.

The Pope: Concerns being able to fit in with, or have peace with family, friends, or community; maximizing predictability in life; gaining education or learning things.

The Lovers: Concerns joining oneself to a person, place, lifestyle, or institution one desires to be joined to. Can refer to couples.

The Chariot: Concerns making progress on one's goals or in one's life generally. Can be concerns about knowing the road ahead. Can also be concerns regarding travel or moving.

Justice: Concerns gaining fair returns for what one has done, or gaining justice for one's experiences. Can refer to legal issues or violations against one's boundaries or person.

The Hermit: Concerns being able to find time for oneself, differentiate oneself, or become a stronger, better person. May concern loneliness or isolation, property or inheritance, or health.

The Wheel of the World: Concerns relating to money, retirement, or long-term financial/personal stability.

Strength: Concerns gaining help one needs for an important task or undertaking, or a sense of greater capability. Can also refer to an important ally.

The Hanged Man: Concerns overcoming emotional distress or personal difficulties that one feels stuck in. Can refer to illness.

Death: Concerns letting go of something one cannot get free of, fears of things changing, coping with new things.

Temperance: Concerns finding a personal balance within one's life as a whole, or finding a needed balanced perspective on something. Can also refer to a very important partner or friend.

The Devil: Concerns dealing with compulsions or addictions, or hard situations that control or compel a person.

The Tower: Concerns dealing with very harsh realities in one's life that torment or disempower. Can be a concern about danger or loss.

The Star: Concerns finding inspiration or guidance towards better things, looking for hope or peace. Can refer to family or relationship issues.

The Moon: Concerns overcoming fears in one's life, or depression or anxiety.

The Sun: Concerns seeking happiness and contentment that may have been elusive before, or to bring about healing in one's life or relations.

Judgement: Concerns looking to re-create oneself or be free of past conditions, ideas, or burdens.

The World: Concerns looking for a place to belong or a sense of real purpose, or a desire to feel affirmed or loved. Can concern all that one has achieved up until this point.

Contemplating the Major Arcana Card Images

The last thing that must be discussed is a few notes regarding how to utilize the 22 images of the Major Arcana for contemplative development and insight. To begin with, one must have read and studied the Narrative of the mysteries given in Chapter One very thoroughly. Beginning with The Fool (or, if you prefer, any card that especially draws your attention or a card randomly drawn) the image is set up before you so that you can gaze very easily upon it in natural light. Contemplation always requires quiet alone time.

These images have the power to unlock deep insights, insights that come from an other-than-rational place. The more one contemplates them, the better one will understand their secret messages in readings, and the better one's soul will become oriented to the deeper meaning of the many situations and experiences we find ourselves facing in life.

The process of contemplation is simplicity itself: when you are ready, and have your peaceful alone-time with the card illuminated before you, you gaze upon it steadily until you can easily see it with your eyes closed. Don't hurry this process- it can take many sessions before you have fully internalized a card in this way. When you can close your eyes and still clearly see the card, imagine that the image in your mind is being seen by you through a window. Open the window and leap into the "world" of the card. You will land right in the center of the image.

The moment your feet touch the ground, you should experience the world of the card in every sensory way you can. If you entered into the world of The Hanged Man, you will see dark, dreary moors stretching out to infinity around you, under the same grey sky you see in the card. You will be standing on one of the roads that make up the crossroads where the man was hanged. And you will see his body hanging there, from the gibbet, perhaps slowly rocking in the wind, making a creaking sound. The simple act of bringing this world to life inside you changes you inside in subtle and important ways.

Look at The Hanged Man and the entire situation. Make it as internally real as you can, and take note of how it makes you feel. There can be no shame, guilt, doubts regarding your feelings; this is the truth of your personal contemplation, whatever it might be. Just remember to keep track of how you feel, and where you feel those things in your body. Your body must always be included in these explorations in this way.

Spend a good bit of time watching the central figure or figures of the card. Let them come to life as far as they can; (The Hanged Man doesn't do much on the gallows but swing there, however the light glowing around his head and that open third eye of his can be worth a look.) Watch what they do. See everything, but don't try to speak to them. If they say something, just listen.

When you are finally ready (and you should take your time here) walk away from the central figure of the card and start exploring the rest of the world of the card. Walk into the dark moors that the Hanged Man sits at the center of. Leave the road and walk around. Focus on the distant horizon. Feel the wind, hear its moan. Look back once you've gone a ways, to see the distant figure of the dead man hanging there. Then just keep experiencing this vast landscape.

The Devil card presents an underground landscape, meaning that you'll be exploring tunnels and caves, which themselves may open into outdoors landscapes. The World card places you floating in a light blue void with the central figure of that card, but the distant borders of that great open space have forests for you to explore.

You are only in this contemplative exercise to *see*- and to hear, smell, taste and touch- but never to verbally interact directly with any other person or being you might encounter. If you do encounter a person, you may see whatever they want to show you, or follow them somewhere so that they can show you other things, but you remain silent and watchful. If you come across a place like an old ruined cottage on the moors of The Hanged Man, you can enter in and look around. Take note of what is there. You can even touch things, but you never verbally interact at any time. Always take deep note of how you feel throughout the experience.

When you are ready to end the contemplation, go back to where the central figure of the card was, and look into the sky or above you. There should be a window floating there, and through it, you should see yourself sitting with your eyes closed. Jump back through and open your eyes.

Over time, it will become very clear to you what kinds of impact this exercise is having, at a subtle level. Do not lose commitment to this practice if you take it up. It is my dearest hope that all of your interactions with the sacred and powerful oracle of Tarot- whether divination or contemplation or both- will yield for you great joy, guidance, and wisdom.

Even when the oracle challenges you or disappoints your hopes, I hope that you will continue to treat it with respect and remember that it exists like a person of its own, and no other person in our lives ever behaves just as we wish they would. This person will always be a good counselor and guide to you if you approach it properly and remember your limitations and biases as a human person living in a very hard human world.

About The Author

Robin Artisson lives along the forested and rocky coast of Maine and devotes his time to the study of spiritual ecology and folk sorcery. He is a member of Covenant DeSavyok, a working group devoted to exploring the Unseen world through the lens of local spirit-relations and folkloric metaphysics. Robin has been a diviner for many years, focusing most of his effort on Cartomancy, lot-casting, dream incubation, and sortilege. He is the author of several books on the pre-Industrial origins of Witchcraft, Pre-Christian spirituality, and mythology.

Made in the USA
Middletown, DE
22 June 2017